Foster Home Breal

The Practice of Social Work
General Editors: Bill Jordan and Jean Packman

Foster Home Breakdown

DAVID BERRIDGE
and
HEDY CLEAVER

Basil Blackwell

First published 1987
First published in USA 1988

Basil Blackwell Ltd
108 Cowley Road, Oxford, OX4 1JF, UK

Basil Blackwell Inc.
432 Park Avenue South, Suite 1503
New York, NY 10016, USA

British Library Cataloguing in Publication Data

Berridge, David
    Foster home breakdown—(The Practice
    of social work; v.16).
    1. Foster home care
    I. Title   II. Cleaver, Hedy   III. Series
    362.7′33   HV875

ISBN 0–631–15817–0
ISBN 0–631–15916–9 Pbk

Typeset in 11 on 12½pt Times Roman
by Alan Sutton Publishing, Gloucester
Printed in Great Britain by Billing & Sons Ltd, Worcester

Contents

Acknowledgements

Looking back on a research study, for us at least, resurrects many pleasant memories. Numerous people have unselfishly given their time and this book is only possible because of their generosity.

Most importantly, we are grateful to the Economic and Social Research Council for funding the research. We are also indebted to personnel in the three study agencies who assisted us in collecting the necessary information: managers, social workers, administrative assistants, foster parents, residential workers, teachers and – last but by no means least – young people in care and their parents. There are so many personalities who come to mind, it would be inconsiderate to name only a few.

Several people kindly offered to read sections of this book in draft form: Ramona Foley, Barbara Kahan, Jean Packman, Roy Parker, Christine Reeves, Jane Rowe and John Triseliotis. Their observations were most helpful, but we should add, however, that any shortcomings remain our responsibility. Mike Little provided invaluable computing and statistical assistance, and we were further aided in the production of the manuscript by Mike Kelly and Margot Blake at the Dartington Social Research Unit and by Melanie Dinemuro and Sarah Dudley at the National Children's Bureau.

Research is an activity that entails contact with a broad range of people yet, paradoxically, it can also be a lonely and isolating experience. We are particularly grateful, therefore, for the support that was always forthcoming from our research colleagues: especially Spencer Millham, Roger Bullock, Ken Hosie and Mike Little at Dartington; Roy Parker at the University of Bristol; and Ron Davie and Elsa Ferri at the National Children's Bureau.

David Berridge
Hedy Cleaver

1
Introduction

Children in care are constantly in the news. Whereas the situation of the poorest sections of our society receives scant attention, the rearing of their young paradoxically arouses considerable moral indignation and an urge to intervene. One can rarely sit through a news bulletin or scan the pages of the daily press without discovering an admonishment of social workers for their alleged mishandling of a child care case. On some occasions, we are exposed to the horrific details of ill-treatment and to castigations of social workers for failing to remove the child from home. Yet much of this criticism is inconsistent, for when children and families have actually been separated, social services are vulnerable to equally vociferous attacks for acting precipitately and violating parents' and children's rights.

Debates over the precise circumstances in which social workers should intervene in that most cherished of institutions, the family, rely on a number of assumptions. Can, for example, the state, in the form of local government bureaucracies, actually 'parent', particularly in the long-term? It is well established from numerous research studies that children admitted to local authority care emanate from situations of extreme adversity: their households have been affected by poverty, unemployment, single parenthood and poor housing conditions; parental illness, both mental and physical, is not uncommon.[1] Frequently – and not surprisingly in such circumstances – standards of parenting are deemed to be unsatisfactory. Yet, as this book will reveal, when social workers become involved in family problems which require one or more children to enter local authority 'care', the alternative experience too often proves to be neither as enriching nor stable as one would wish. Indeed, as a recent study of the child care system has shown, social services intervention can have adverse effects, leading unintentionally to children becoming isolated and bereft of family and other social contact.[2]

This book focuses on one of the most significant parts of our child welfare system – foster care – and examines the experience of children placed in other families with foster parents. More specifically, it concentrates on the further disruption caused to children when foster placements break down. As we shall see in the following chapters, placement breakdown is regrettably not infrequent and serious damage to children can result. Before examining this problem in detail, we must first place it in its broader context.

In recent years, critics of services for children in care have tended to highlight the deficiencies of *residential* rather than foster care and, following the writings of a number of distinguished authors including Bowlby[3] and Goffman[4], most commentators have concluded that residential institutions are unsatisfactory environments in which to rear children. It is alleged that they fail to achieve desired changes in behaviour and are inordinately expensive.[5] Admittedly, it requires a certain stretch of the imagination to believe that children's homes and other institutions are providing – or, indeed, should *seek* to provide – specialized 'treatment' for children, in a context in which some 80 per cent of residential child care workers are professionally unqualified. Nevertheless, as research has demonstrated, groups of residential institutions continue to play an important part in the child care system, particularly for adolescents, and are closely integrated with other forms of intervention.[6] Indeed, a recent nationwide survey of children's homes, undertaken by the DHSS Social Services Inspectorate, although critical of certain shortcomings of the residential sector, confirmed that most children were appropriately placed.[7]

In contrast to this prevalent, somewhat negative approach towards residence, foster care is currently on the crest of a wave. Whether this stems from a perceived greater effectiveness or parsimony is unclear; more likely, it is a combination of the two. Nevertheless, family placements are becoming increasingly popular options for children entering care. Indeed, as national child care statistics reveal, increasing proportions of children in local authority care are now being placed with foster parents rather than in residential setting. For example, table 1.1 indicates that, over a 5-year period

TABLE 1.1 PLACEMENTS OF CHILDREN IN CARE IN ENGLAND AND WALES IN 1979 AND 1984

| | 1979 | | 1984 | |
Placements	*(no.)*	*(%)*	*(no.)*	*(%)*
Fostered with non-relatives	29,000	29	32,500	42
Fostered with relatives	6,800	7	4,800	6
Residential care – local authority and voluntary agencies	34,600	35	18,400	24
In the care of a parent, guardian, relative or friend	18,700	19	13,500	18
Other placements	11,000	11	7,600	10
Total in care[a]	100,100		76,800	

[a] The total number of children in care will be an underestimate as not all authorities submitted statistical returns.

Sources: Department of Health and Social Security, *Children in Care of Local Authorities, Year Ending 31 March 1984, England*, DHSS, 1986; *Children in Care in England and Wales, March 1979*, DHSS, 1981. Welsh Office, *Children in Care or Under Supervision Orders in Wales: Year Ended 31 March 1985*, Welsh Office, 1986.

between 1979 and 1984 (the most recent for which statistics are available), the number of children in care in England and Wales who, at any one time, are sheltered in residential settings diminished by 16,000. In contrast, during the same period, the number fostered rose by 1,500. Against the background of a declining number of children in care, this change represents an increase from 36 per cent to 48 per cent of children living in foster homes. Significantly, the growth has concerned children fostered with non-relatives (or 'strangers', using the term non-pejoratively), whereas the use of fostering with relatives has reduced slightly. We shall return to this issue in a subsequent chapter. However, it is interesting to note that the relative decline in the use of fostering with relatives – a trend that has continued over a number of years – is curious in view of the research evidence which suggests its effectiveness.[8] While foster care expands, residential care is currently in the doldrums with establishments throughout the country continuing to close.

Background to the study

This study of fostering breakdowns developed from a previous research investigation undertaken by one of the authors. Between 1981 and 1983 a comparative study was made of 20 children's homes. The research was conducted during a period in which opinions opposing residential care were strong and in which resources were increasingly directed towards fostering. In this context, findings from the study of children's homes proved to be somewhat controversial. In contrast to much previous institutional research, the children's homes were discovered to be making a significant contribution to child care services and some of the establishments intensively studied were impressive. Furthermore, an important finding from the children's homes study concerned the interdependence between these institutions and fostering. The children's homes were discovered not only to be preparing a significant minority of children – approximately 35 per cent – for moves *into* foster homes but also to be accepting *back* into residence many whose fosterings had failed. Indeed, the size of the group falling into this second category was unexpected: 33 per cent of all residents living in the 20 homes studied had experienced breakdowns in planned long-term foster placements, including 12 per cent who had witnessed two or more.[9]

These fostering failures posed difficulties for residential staff: the experience of a fostering breakdown was disturbing for most children; staff and social workers were often unsure about how best to proceed in planning for the child's future. The implications of a failed fostering were summarized in this earlier research as follows:

It is very important not to underestimate the effects of a fostering breakdown on a child . . . Clearly, foster breakdowns are highly disruptive and emotionally distressing. They disintegrate peer and other social networks, wrench children from familiar neighbourhoods and lead to a change of school. Such precipitate transfers shatter the fragile trust the children have in the permanence of adult relationships, resurrect memories they have of earlier separations and encourage emotional disturbance and learned indifference. Residential staff often describe children who have recently experienced foster breakdowns as 'emotionally shattered'. Teachers also report that such children frequently function well below their potential for several years following the disruption.[10]

Thus, while the majority of children in care undoubtedly benefit from their experience of fostering, there is an important minority whose progress is hampered by further disruptions in their care careers; a group whom this study seeks to help.

Criticism of existing fostering services also came in a report from the DHSS Social Services Inspectorate, which undertook a wide-ranging study of the subject. While acknowledging many innovative and exciting developments occurring in some areas, as with the Inspectorate's investigation of children's homes referred to earlier, the report also highlighted a number of deficiencies. At times departing perceptibly from the customary, neutral Civil Service style, the conclusions of the study are unequivocal:

. . . It is apparent from this report that there is no room for complacency; almost every aspect of fostering practice is criticised. Visits to children who were boarded-out were either delayed or missed, statutory requirements for medical examination were neglected, schooling did not feature as important and reports and reviews were not made as they should have been. There was widespread disregard of the Boarding-Out of Children Regulations, which prescribe minimum standards of practice that must be adhered to in the selection of foster parents, the placement and visiting of children, the reviewing of their situation and the writing of reports. Children in care who were boarded-out received less attention than other children in care, less attention than the minimum requirements of the statutory regulations and less attention than the objective reality that their situation warranted. These omissions in the care of children arise from deficiencies in policy, management, supervision and social work practice.[11]

Thus, despite the widespread popularity of fostering, an authoritative report made a number of trenchant criticisms of present services. It is significant to note, however, that the degree of concern expressed appears to have had little impact on the vigour with which fostering policies were pursued or the rate at which residential facilities continued to close.

Further evidence of the efficacy of different types of substitute care was contained in empirical research undertaken by the Dartington Social Research Unit, which focused over a two-year period on the experiences of a cohort of 450 children admitted to local authority care in 1980 in five local authorities in England and Wales.[12] Among its other findings, this study revealed the highly precarious nature of many placements of children in care. Presumably, by deciding to intervene, Social Services Departments were intending to offer a more stable and rewarding alternative to what children had previously experienced. Yet, if one traces the care experiences of the 450 children, this was by no means guaranteed and placement transfer was not uncommon. For example, of the long-stay children who remained in care for two years, almost three-fifths had lived in three or more placements, including 14 per cent who had experienced at least five. Some of these moves occurred for administrative reasons, such as transferring from one short-stay foster home to another or moving out of an observation and assessment centre; nevertheless, no fewer than *40* per cent of the 170 children who were still in care after two years had witnessed a breakdown of a placement. Significantly, all types of placement were prone to abrupt termination. However, as table 1.2 reveals, fosterings were particularly vulnerable.

TABLE 1.2 PROPORTION OF PREMATURE PLACEMENT BREAKDOWN WITHIN A COHORT OF 170 CHILDREN STILL IN CARE AFTER TWO YEARS (INCLUDING ONGOING PLACEMENTS)

Type of placement	*% breaking down*
Foster home (non-relatives)	34
'Independent living' situations	28
At home or 'home on trial'	23
Community home with education (CHE)	24
Children's home	17
Home with observation and assessment	12
All placements	21

Table 1.2 demonstrates that 34 per cent of fosterings broke down over the two-year period in comparison with 21 per cent of all placements. However, two observations need to be made concerning these figures. First, the rates are

obviously an underestimate as some of the current place-ments will break down in the future. Second, these findings must be interpreted cautiously: although it may appear that fostering is twice as unstable as placements in children's homes, it must be emphasized that residential placements are more likely to end for reasons *other* than breakdown, such as for the administrative reasons previously mentioned. Hence, the follow-up study confirms that placement instability is a general feature of the child care system and is not restricted to particular types of intervention. Naturally, different breakdown experiences will have a varied impact on children and the evidence from the cohort study on the precipitate termination of fosterings is disconcerting. For example, children are propelled into residential care, schooling is disrupted and links with families become more difficult to sustain.

In addition to providing statistical material, the cohort study of 450 children is also useful in suggesting hypotheses for investigation concerning the problem of fostering breakdown. In particular, the study suggested that features of the placement itself were more significant for understan-ding placement breakdown than were characteristics of the child and his or her family. Furthermore, simple instru-mental factors – such as distance between placement and home – proved to be insufficient for explaining observed patterns of breakdown. Instead, more attention needed to be focused on placement dynamics such as the interactions and negotiations between the participants and their adjust-ments over time. These considerations have influenced the theoretical orientation of this research, which is laid out in the following chapter.

Thus, we have seen that there are three distinct influences which have encouraged us to explore further the problem of fostering breakdown. First, a study of children's homes demonstrated that a significant number of fostering failures were being sheltered by the residential sector and that these posed particular problems for staff. Second, a DHSS report was critical of the organisation and quality of fostering services; and, finally, recent empirical research demonstrated a high degree of placement instability for children in care.

Other studies of fostering breakdown

On consulting the relevant literature to discover what studies had been undertaken on the problem of fostering breakdown, it soon became apparent that, in contrast to other child care services such as adoption and residential care, relatively little recent research had been mounted. There were, however, some notable exceptions and these will now be discussed.

A useful starting point for any researcher interested in fostering is Rowe's work. Her and her colleagues' most recent study of long-term foster care is one of the most significant books on child care to be published in recent years.[13] As its title implies and as the authors acknowledge, however, the study is actually not concerned with long-term fostering in general but is about *successful* long-term fostering. The sample of 200 placements under scrutiny was selected on the basis that they had each endured for at least three years.

Nevertheless, Rowe's research reveals a number of interesting findings. For example, long-term fostering was found to be making an important contribution to child care services but Rowe and her colleagues questioned whether the security it provides for children and foster parents is adequate. In addition, the researchers discovered that an 'exclusive' model of fostering predominates: that is where foster parents discourage any sharing of care with children's own families and social workers and, instead, perceive their own role to be akin to that of a natural parent.[14]

Another finding of particular significance for the present study concerns the age at which children in Rowe's sample were initially placed in their foster home. On investigation, it was discovered that half of the children were aged under two at the time of placement and a further third were between two and four. Thus, barely one child in six was of school age; a low proportion in comparison with other studies that will be discussed later in this chapter. The somewhat disconcerting conclusion to be drawn from this evidence is that few foster placements involving children of school age endure; or, alternatively, as the authors euphemistically phrase it 'Most of the children who were over five when placed by the project authorities must have fallen by the wayside.'[15] This finding balances the generally optimistic tone of the book.

Research that has focused specifically on the problem of breakdown in foster care consists broadly of two types: these can be termed 'predictive' and 'intensive' studies.

'Predictive' studies

The first group of studies are those that seek to establish predictive factors that are associated with placement outcome. These investigations also calculate breakdown rates and have revealed consistently that approximately half of all planned long-term foster placements break down prematurely within periods ranging from between two and five years. This evidence is complemented by research focusing on foster parents who cease to foster. Jones, for example, discovered that some 40 per cent of new foster parents decided to discontinue fostering within a year.[16] As Prosser has observed, however, although there is broad consensus over the *degree* of instability, the search for reliable indicators of outcome has been less fruitful. Indeed, many previous findings are contradictory.[17]

The most significant of the predictive studies are those by Trasler, Parker and George and, because of their importance, each investigation will be discussed in turn. The first of these inquiries – *In Place of Parents* – was undertaken by Trasler and published in 1960.[18] His research, based in one Children's Department, traced the experiences of a sample of 138 children who were fostered. The study group consisted of 57 whose placements had 'broken down' over a 3-year survey period and a control group of a further 81 children, who were deemed to be satisfactorily placed.

Trasler revealed that terminations in placements tended to occur early on, with the first two years of a fostering being particularly vulnerable; indeed, three-quarters of all breakdowns took place within this period. Four key variables were found by Trasler to be significantly related to outcome. First, the early rearing history of a child was important and placement failure was more likely to be experienced by children who had been separated from their parents during infancy and lived during this period in a residential setting. Second, Trasler reported that successful fostering was inversely related to age of the child: placements involving older children were more likely to end prematurely than those involving their younger counterparts. Furthermore, two placement-related factors were found to be important. These were the age of the foster mother at the time of placement (women under forty witnessed a disproportionately high number of breakdowns) and the 'family dynamics' in the foster home, particularly concerning the presence of other children. Trasler demonstrated that failure rates were noticeably higher when foster parents had a child of their own who was of the same sex and within three years of age of the foster child. It is also interesting to note that the most favourable circumstances were those where *another* foster child, either related or unrelated, was present in the household. These situations proved twice as successful as those where there was no other child present at all, or where the only other children were those of the foster parents.

Six years after Trasler's research, Parker, in his study *Decision in Child Care*,[19] developed further the objective assessment of foster care and the search for predictive factors. Parker's investigation remains, more than twenty years after it was written, probably the most influential study of foster breakdown and is regularly alluded to in discussions and reports by social workers. However, as we shall see, when moving from the planning stage to actual placement of a foster child, the research messages are, unfortunately, frequently disregarded.

As with Trasler's study, Parker based his research on social workers' records in one Children's Department and examined retrospectively over a five-year period the care experiences of a sample of 209 children living in planned long-stay foster placements. Comparing placements that survived for five years with those that did not, he discovered a 'success rate' of 52 per cent. Parker explored a variety of factors that were associated with outcome and concluded that six were paramount. First was the age at which a foster child was separated from its mother: the later this separation occurred, the poorer was the prognosis for the fostering. Second was the foster child's previous life history; fosterings were discovered to be particularly successful when the child had previously undergone a family placement, especially if the first had been positive. In addition, a *brief* interlude in residential care in infancy was also found to be associated with successful outcomes; but if this lasted more than three years it had the reverse effect. The third of Parker's six key findings was that a natural mother's death prior to fostering is closely linked to subsequent fostering breakdown. Fourth, as with Trasler, the age of child at the time of placement was related to outcome: the likelihood of successful fostering decreased with age. Fifth, children who posed behaviour problems were more likely to experience a placement breakdown than those who did not. Finally, Parker highlighted the significance of the presence of other children in the foster household. The probability of failure was increased where foster parents had children of their own, particularly if they were younger than five or similar in age to the foster child.

The third of the major predictive studies of foster placement outcome is George's *Foster Care: Theory and Practice*.[20] George gathered data on 128 children in three Children's Departments and, defining 'success' as placements that lasted for five years, the overall 'success rate' was found to be lower than Parker's at 40 per cent. The rates for the three departments in which the research was based were remarkably similar, at 43 per cent, 40 per cent and 38 per cent. George's study revealed seven factors that were strongly associated with outcome – some, but not all, of which were also highlighted in Trasler's and Parker's research. The seven variables that heralded foster placement breakdowns were: children's origin from families which had a history of intervention from welfare agencies, particularly the NSPCC; the *older* the child when separated from its mother; the *older* the child at the time of placement; separation of siblings in care between placements; the *younger* the age of the foster mother; the presence of foster parents' own children, regardless of age; and, finally, and interestingly, *similarities* in religious faith between foster parents and foster child.

It is apparent that the three major predictive studies of Trasler, Parker and George show agreement in a number of areas, yet their results are by no means conclusive. For example, their findings concerning breakdown rates in long-term fosterings are broadly consistent and a failure rate of approximately half was discovered in each investigation. The three authors also revealed that placement breakdown was more likely to affect older children and to occur in a context in which foster parents' *own* children were present, particularly if they were of a similar age to the foster child. Beyond this, however, consensus was lacking and findings concerning one area – age at which the foster child was first separated from its family – are directly contradictory.

These landmarks in child care research have been supplemented by other, smaller-scale investigations. Napier, for example, studied fostering breakdown in a Children's Department in the north-west of England and disclosed a failure rate, over five years, of 37 per cent.[21] More optimistically, Aldgate and Hawley discovered that 80 per cent of their sample in Oxford were still in placements after two years.[22] Furthermore, it is interesting to note that the problem of placement stability does not appear to be a uniquely British phenomenon and Kraus and Fanshel, for example, have identified similar problems in Australia and the US respectively.[23]

'Intensive' studies

In contrast to those investigations which have sought to quantify the level of breakdown in foster care and to establish predictive factors, a second group of relevant studies – few in number – are those which are 'intensive' and concentrate attention on the experience of participants in the fostering process: foster parents, foster children, social workers and, less frequently, natural parents. A particularly important recent study in this tradition is that of Aldgate and Hawley, which will be discussed in chapter 8.[24] At a more general level, the publications of Kahan[25] and the *Who Cares?* group[26] are valuable. These demonstrate that the long-term problems experienced by children who have been fostered are necessarily no less severe than those of their peers who lived in residential establishments. Moreover, a broad study of children admitted to local authority care has shown that natural parents feel excluded from placements – both foster and residential – and find the experience of visiting highly stressful. Consequently, most stop visiting or stay away altogether.[27]

Studies concentrating specifically on foster care have supported these findings. Rowe, for example, whose work on long-term fostering we have already encountered, revealed the exclusion of natural parents from the care of their children.[28] In addition, Thorpe has confirmed that original parents feel tacitly excluded by social workers from the care process. Her research, involving interviews with social workers and foster children, concluded that children's 'well-being', as rated by their social workers, was enhanced if the following three conditions were fulfilled: first, that the child has a good understanding of his or her foster situation; second, that the child identifies primarily with its natural parents; and, finally, that the child is in regular contact with its parents.[29]

One of the most significant findings from the intensive research into foster care concerns what can be termed the 'role ambiguity' of foster parents: that is, that foster parents occupy a 'parental' role but are not actually the 'real' – or biological – parents of the child. We shall see in the following chapters that foster children can experience considerable conflicts when foster parents assume the role of natural parents and attenuate their temporary status. Indeed, Shaw and his colleagues have affirmed that the majority of foster parents do not differentiate perceptibly between their own role and that of a natural parent.[30] The practical implications of this have been discussed by Triseliotis, who concluded that the most accomplished foster parents are those with warm and open personalities; who demonstrate stability in their own lives and social relationships; and – very importantly – are not antipathetic to references to the child's family of origin. Less successful foster households, in contrast, lack the same degree of warmth and consistency; contain relationship problems, low levels of tolerance, and tension associated with financial, accommodation and other problems.[31]

Having briefly discussed the two broad groups of studies in foster care research – that is 'predictive' studies and those of a more 'intensive' nature – a number of general conclusions can be drawn. The current study of fostering breakdown has been designed to attempt to rectify some of the gaps in knowledge; four deficiencies are apparent in the existing literature.

First, much of the research is now out of date. The predictive studies, in particular, were conducted some 20 years ago, and, clearly, much has changed in social services since the 1960s. Rowe and her colleagues' research, as we have already emphasised, provides invaluable contemporary material but their focus of attention was very specific.

A second observation on the existing literature is that research has rarely incorporated a comparative dimension but, instead, is usually undertaken in only one locality. It is also typically based on social workers' records; obviously, these would portray foster care from a particular perspective and provide only a partial account.

Third, it is important to recognize that virtually all previous fostering research has focused exclusively on planned *long-term* placements. Alternatively, for example, there is remarkably little known about the impact of *short-term* fostering, which is experienced each year by large numbers of younger children. Similarly new styles of fostering, such as 'intermediate' placements, and new issues, including transracial fostering, are hitherto relatively unexplored.

Finally, much existing research is limited in its theoretical orientation and, more specifically, there is a dearth of intensive, qualitative material; a point stressed by Prosser in her overview of foster care research, when she asserts that very little is known about what *actually* happens in foster homes.[32] Furthermore, Triseliotis has observed that a neglected course of enquiry is the examination of the *interaction* between participants in the fostering process, including foster parents, foster children and natural parents. This would be expected to reveal useful information on the circumstances precipitating placement breakdown, while it would also be interesting to examine the subsequent effects on those involved.[33]

Research questions

Having examined the existing literature on foster care and suggested some of its deficiencies, we shall now identify the main questions to be addressed in this study. The following chapter contains a more detailed discussion of some of the theoretical and methodological issues involved; however, it may be useful at this stage to lay out briefly what the major concerns are to be.

An important area of investigation will be to explore the current incidence of foster home breakdowns. Initially, we must clarify what is meant by 'breakdown' and how it can be measured. Furthermore, is the level of disruption now significantly lower than that discovered twenty years ago before Social Services Departments were established? What are the relative 'success' and 'failure' rates of different types of fostering, such as planned long-term and short-term fostering, fostering with relatives and other types of placement? Do breakdown rates differ between agencies?

We shall also investigate the causes of placement breakdown. Are there different types of ending and what are the contributory factors? Can one predict with any degree of certainty the likely outcome of a placement, or is planning more hazardous? Can the premature breakdown of a foster placement be attributed essentially to the problems posed by a child's behaviour, or are family dynamics in the foster household and other placement-related factors more significant? In addition, what do each of the participants in the fostering process perceive to be the salient factors?

In addition, the research will explore subsequent strategies employed by social workers and others to remedy the problems associated with placement breakdown. We shall also explore how the participants are subsequently affected. What happens to children thereafter?

Obviously, we cannot hope to provide definitive answers to all of these questions. Our aim is to provide information to facilitate future discussion and research. In conclusion, therefore, it is intended that the study should make a contribution at three distinct levels. First, at a conceptual level, we aim to refine the concept and measurement of 'breakdown'. Second, in theoretical terms, the research will seek to complement an 'extensive', statistical survey with an 'intensive' investigation, which explores what actually occurs in a sample of foster placements. This will compare the perceptions and explanations of participants as to why breakdown occurred. Finally, the study seeks to provide fresh empirical information on a subject

currently of great concern to many Social Services
Departments.

We end this opening chapter by briefly referring to one
other important issue. In the turbulent times of the 1960s,
the influential American sociologist, Howard Becker, posed
the question 'Whose Side Are We On?' and argued that
social scientists should make their value positions explicit.[34]
In exploring aspects of political sociology, for example, it
may be possible for researchers to admit that their allegience
lies with certain social groups rather than others. For those
of us involved in evaluative studies of social work services,
however, the situation is rather more complex and it would
be somewhat oversimplistic, to say the least, to assert that
one is a proponent of certain types of intervention rather
than others. Nevertheless, child care services over the years
have been characterized by swings in policy and some
individuals and pressure groups are strong advocates of
particular approaches, such as fostering, residential care or
adoption.

It may be helpful to emphasize at the outset, therefore,
that because the focus of our research is on fostering
breakdown, it does not signify that we are unduly pessimistic
or, in any way, 'anti-fostering'. Indeed, as we shall see, most
foster placements have satisfactory outcomes and we would
wish to see as many children in care as possible placed in
appropriate foster homes. However, although most fosterings proceed to plan, a significant minority do not and
further damage to a child can ensue. Hence, in the following
chapters we seek to provide relevant information for policy
makers and practitioners in order to make child care services
more effective.

Notes

1 See for example: R. Parker ed *Caring for Separated Children*,
   Macmillan, 1980.
2 S. Millham, R. Bullock, K. Hosie and M. Haak, *Lost in Care:*

The Problems of Maintaining Links between Children in Care and their Families, Gower, 1986.

3 J. Bowlby, *Maternal Care and Mental Health*, World Health Organisation Monograph Series No. 2, WHO, 1952.

4 E. Goffman, *Asylums: Essays on the Social Situation of Mental Patients and Other Inmates*, Doubleday, 1961.

5 For example R. Clarke and D. Cornish, *Residential Treatment and its Effects on Delinquency*, Home Office Research Studies No. 32, HMSO, 1975; Department of the Environment, *The Provision of Child Care: A Study at Eight Local Authorities in England and Wales*, Department of the Environment, 1981.

6 D. Berridge, *Children's Homes*, Basil Blackwell, 1985.

7 Department of Health and Social Security, Social Services Inspectorate, *Inspection of Community Homes*, DHSS, 1985.

8 J. Rowe, H. Cain, M. Hundleby and A. Keane, *Long-Term Foster Care*, Batsford, 1984.

9 Berridge, *Children's Homes*.

10 Ibid., p. 41.

11 Department of Health and Social Security, Social Work Service, *A Study of the Boarding-Out of Children*, DHSS, 1981, pp. 25, 26.

12 Millham et al., *Lost in Care*.

13 Rowe et al., *Long-Term Foster Care*.

14 See R. Holman, 'The place of fostering in social work', *British Journal of Social Work*, vol. 5, no. 1, 1975, pp. 3–29.

15 Rowe et al., *Long-Term Foster Care*, p. 28.

16 E. Jones, *Portsmouth Fostering Study*, Social Research and Intelligence Unit, 1973.

17 H. Prosser, *Perspectives on Foster Care*, National Children's Bureau and NFER, 1978.

18 G. Trasler, *In Place of Parents*, Routledge and Kegan Paul, 1960.

19 R. Parker, *Decision in Child Care*, Allen and Unwin, 1966.

20 V. George, *Foster Care: Theory and Practice*, Routledge and Kegan Paul, 1970.

21 H. Napier, 'Success and failure in foster care', *British Journal of Social Work*, vol. 2, no. 2, 1972, pp. 187–204.

22 J. Aldgate and D. Hawley, 'Helping foster families through disruption', *Adoption and Fostering*, vol. 10, no. 2, 1986, pp. 44–9.

23 J. Kraus, 'Predicting success of foster placements for school

age children', *Social Work*, vol. 16, no. 1, 1971, pp. 63–72; D. Fanshel and E. Shinn, *Children in Foster Care*, Columbia, 1978.

24   Aldgate and Hawley, 'Helping foster families through disruption'.

25   B. Kahan, *Growing Up in Care*, Basil Blackwell, 1979.

26   R. Page and G. Clark eds, *Who Cares? Young People in Care Speak Out*, National Children's Bureau, 1977.

27   Millham et al., *Lost in Care*.

28   Rowe et al., *Long-Term Foster Care*.

29   See R. Thorpe, 'The experience of children and parents living apart: implications and guidelines for practice', in J. Triseliotis ed., *New Developments in Foster Care and Adoption*, Routledge and Kegan Paul, 1980.

30   M. Shaw, K. Lebens and A. Cosh, *Children Between Families, Summary Report of a Study of Foster Home Care at the Introduction of the Children Bill 1974*, University of Leicester School of Social Work, 1975.

31   J. Triseliotis, 'Growing up in foster care and after', in J. Triseliotis ed, *New Developments in Foster Care and Adoption*, Routledge and Kegan Paul, 1980.

32   Prosser, *Perspectives on Foster Care*.

33   J. Triseliotis, 'Growing up in foster care and after'.

34   H. Becker, 'Whose side are we on?, *Social Problems*, vol. 14, 1967, pp. 239–47.

2

Theory, Concepts and Methodology

Theoretical issues

This study, the reader will be relieved to discover, is not a theoretical treatise. It is written from a predominantly sociological viewpoint but utilizes theory to provide insight and coherence to our understanding of fostering practice, rather than the reverse – that is, using empirical material to develop theory. Before outlining the research design and presenting findings, it is first necessary to raise some theoretical and conceptual issues surrounding the investigation.

The research incorporates both *extensive* and *intensive* dimensions. The *extensive* approach consists of a survey, from social work records in three contrasting agencies, of a large sample of foster placements – in total, 530 fosterings experienced by 372 children (some had more than one placement). This extensive component follows the tradition of the 'predictive' studies discussed in the previous chapter, and seeks to provide up-to-date information on the incidence of breakdowns in fostering of various types and the associated factors. Hence, findings from earlier studies are re-examined but fresh hypotheses have led to other areas of inquiry being included. In order to facilitate statistical analysis, the extensive survey has employed a large study population. However, unless one is flanked by a platoon of research interviewers, 'coders' and computer programmers, the amount of information that can be gathered on each case will inevitably be limited. For this reason, this broad view of the state of the art of foster care was complemented by a more detailed scrutiny, described later in this chapter, of a small sample of placements.

In addition to examining the comparative rates of foster placement breakdown in the study areas, three perspectives influenced the organization of material gathered for the extensive survey. These were particularly relevant when exploring the factors associated with breakdown.

First, an important influence on the 1960s fostering studies – and, indeed, on social work more generally – was the work of Bowlby and the 'maternal deprivation' thesis.[1] Bowlby emphasized the significance of the mother-child bond, particularly in the first three years of a child's life. If this relationship was unsatisfactory, or if separation occurred during this crucial period, Bowlby asserted that serious psychological problems could ensue. Since publication some 40 years ago, Bowlby's work has not only generated considerable interest but also attracted criticism, leading to modifications in the original concept which have emphasized the sociological aspects of separation.[2] Nevertheless, one does not have to support fully the psychoanalytic tradition to hold the view that, other things being equal, children appear to benefit if there is continuity in upbringing, especially during the early years. Hence – and in order to enable comparisons with previous research – we shall explore the early rearing histories of fostered children and relate this to outcome. We shall also examine the impact of children's care careers, particularly the way in which a child's introduction to the foster home is managed.

A second perspective influencing the material gathered in the extensive survey concerns the relationship between placement stability and the maintenance of children's social networks. Recent research has demonstrated that admission to local authority care can lead to children's isolation from social support systems,[3] while studies of the problems confronting adolescents leaving care at 18 have highlighted the deleterious effects resulting from the absence of social networks.[4] We shall, therefore, examine foster children's links with their families of origin, together with social workers' efforts in this direction and the impact of these on children's care careers. However, there are dangers in adopting too condescending a view of children and assuming – as does much social work literature – that children's relationships with *adults* are all that matters. Indeed, as other research has indicated, *peer* relationships – such as those with siblings or schoolfriends – are also significant and, for this reason, we shall examine their relationship with placement outcome.[5]

The third perspective guiding the extensive survey was mentioned in the opening chapter and concerns the significance of what can be termed 'placement-related' factors. In contrast to studies of outcome which concentrate exclusively on foster children, we shall also explore characteristics of the foster *household* in which the child lives. Overemphasis on 'supply-side' factors has proved controversial in the study of economics; we anticipate, however, that an examination of this dimension in this field of social research will prove fruitful.

Clearly, the 'extensive' survey, based on social workers' casenotes, and thus perceptions, can only provide a partial view of what happens in foster homes. Hence, we have incorporated a second dimension in the research, namely an intensive approach. Of the four focal points of this study outlined in the previous chapter – that is the incidence, causes, effects and management of fostering breakdowns – the 'extensive' analysis would be expected to provide substantial material on the first and last of these areas. The causes and effects of fostering breakdowns, however, can be more adequately explored by a more detailed, intensive approach.

An important development in sociology has been the influence of phenomenology.[6] This perspective has developed as a response to what is viewed as an overdeterministic approach of other, more positivist, theories. The phenomenological perspective emphasizes the interpretations, negotiations and adaptations of individuals rather than the 'external' determinants of behaviour. Thus, this tradition is a form of 'subjective' sociology. It analyses behaviour at the 'micro' rather than the 'macro' level – that is, it focuses on individuals' interpretations and interactions with others rather than institutions or social structures – and has, clearly, had a considerable impact on empirical research; most notably, perhaps, on the 'interactionist' studies in deviancy and education but also, increasingly, in social work.

The intensive component of this study of fostering breakdown is influenced by this phenomenological tradition and we have analysed in detail ten placements which broke down prematurely. The perspectives, expectations and adjustments of participants in the fostering process were explored in individual interviews and the different interpretations of each situation have been contrasted. In addition, the negotiations that preceded the breakdown have been carefully charted.

The extensive and intensive components of the research are designed to be complementary. The latter not only provides illustrative material for the statistical data; it also leads to fresh insights. For example social workers, foster parents or children may identify key factors of which researchers were unaware when framing their hypotheses and transforming them into elaborate questionnaires and other research instruments. Moreover, although it is rarely admitted, intensive material provides a 'richness' that can otherwise be absent from a research report. A photograph or a few sentences from a child in care can sometimes offer as much insight as pages of detailed analysis and we shall draw on quotations from the subjects of our research.

We make no apologies for adopting what is an eclectic approach. While this stance may displease ideological purists, we would add that despite many years of searching we are yet to discover a unidimensional theoretical view which, in isolation, enables a satisfactory understanding of the operation of child care services. Furthermore, there is still a need in child care research for pioneering empirical studies: we simply do not know, for example, what sorts of children live in foster homes, how long they remain there and the extent to which their experience is satisfactory. Thus, if by drawing on a range of complementary theoretical and methodological approaches we provide material to facilitate discussion of child care policy and practice, as well as guiding future researchers, our aims will have been met.

Conceptual issues

This study also seeks to develop a number of conceptual issues and it is to these that we now turn. In contrast to most previous evaluative studies of the area, this research does not merely concentrate on planned long-term placements but, instead, encompasses a broad range of fosterings. Recent years have witnessed significant initiatives in foster care and it is important for research to reflect, and assist in monitoring, these developments.

Our research focuses, therefore, on four types of foster placements. First, we examine *long-term* fostering, which has traditionally been the cornerstone of this form of substitute family care. Long-term fostering is usually indefinite in its anticipated duration but, for the purposes of the present research, is defined as having been planned to last at least three years. Some local authorities are now moving away from open-ended fosterings and making greater use of adoption, with its added security. The availability of adoption allowances is likely to encourage this development.[7] Furthermore, it will also be interesting to observe the impact on long-term fostering of guardianship procedures; a form of interim legal status introduced in 1985 by the implementation of Section 33 of the Children Act 1975. Yet, despite these recent developments, we shall see in chapter 4 that traditional, long-term fostering still plays a singificant role in child care services.

The second group of placements that we shall examine are planned *short-term* fosterings. The Boarding-Out Regul-ations (the relevant Statutory Instruments that are now being substantially revised for the first time in 30 years) define short-term fostering as that which is intended to last up to eight weeks and we shall stay with this upper limit. This type of placement is experienced mostly by younger children admitted temporarily to local authority care owing to situational problems, such as illness of parent(s) or accommodation difficulties. There are, however, interesting initiatives developing in short-term foster care as an alterna-tive to the more traditional, emergency model and we came across a number of examples. These include the imaginative provision – sometimes on a structured basis – of respite care for families and short-term foster homes being used as a base for the assessment of children's needs and problems. Each year, probably in excess of 10,000 children in England and Wales experience a stay in a short-term foster home and it is quite remarkable that minimal research attention has been given to this very important form of intervention.[8]

The third and fourth types of fosterings which are included in this study are *intermediate* fosterings and '*special family placements*'. As we shall demonstrate in chapter 7, these have a number of features in common. Both tend to be used for older children and/or those who pose particular problems in terms of behaviour, health or physical or mental handicap. In addition, each tend to be planned as medium-term in duration; often envisaged to last between 18 months and a maximum of three years. Intermediate and 'special' placements, in contrast to other fosterings, are also more often contract-based and their objectives tend to be more carefully circumscribed. 'Special' fostering, in particular, is frequently imbued with a more professional, social work orientation and support from social services will be more readily available. Enhanced rates of payment to foster parents is also usual.

Brief reference should also be made to two further types of fosterings that it was decided to exclude from the research. Initially, we intended to gather information on holiday foster placements experienced by children educated in residential schools. However, it soon became apparent that social work casenotes were inadequate for a thorough investigation of the use of this type of placement: the frequency of visits by children to the holiday home was not always recorded; neither was it clear when visiting ceased. Children resident in boarding special schools – especially for those with 'emotional and behavioural' problems – now comprise a small but, nevertheless, significant and *growing* proportion of the total 'in care' population: some 2,100 out of the 79,000 children in care in England and Wales in 1984.[9] By no means all of these schools provide for pupils between terms and it would seem important to know more about the oscillations of children between schools and foster or children's homes, particularly in terms of the degree of continuity and the quality of experience provided.

The exclusion of holiday foster placements was, therefore, involuntary but we decided to disregard from the outset cases in which children were fostered with a view to adoption – that is, by the same couple. The rationale for this is that adoption placements receive a quite different, more intensive, social work service than do those involving fostering. There is a further reason, in a retrospective study of children in care such as this, for excluding placements in which the goal is adoption. Placements that break down in the initial stages will remain in care but those that succeed will leave care on adoption and, hence, may disappear from the sample. There is, therefore, a danger that the fostering breakdown rate is overestimated and it would be interesting to discover whether other retrospective studies have taken account of this eventuality.

Having classified the various types of fostering to be incorporated in the research, we come to a particularly thorny conceptual problem: how to define and measure the outcome of a foster placement. Initially it is clear that, in assessing outcome, there are three major, interrelated considerations. First, there is *duration* – did the placement survive? In order to form a judgement, the length of time a placement is sustained must be compared with the period originally envisaged; the intended duration is not always made explicit. A second factor to take into account concerns the *quality* of the experience: what was the effect, especially on the child, but also on other participants, such as foster parents and the child's family? Finally, another element in evaluating outcome is the extent to which the foster placement *met the social work aims*. Again, complications arise when objectives are not made explicit or if plans change.

Ideally, an evaluation of fostering outcome should comprise a combination of these three elements. Indeed, in our intensive study of a small sample of placements which broke down, we have been able to explore these interrelated issues, including participants' views of the effects on individuals. In our extensive survey, however, owing to limitations of secondary sources of data – in our case, social workers' records – our objectives must, inevitably, be more modest. Hence, the analysis will concentrate on the time dimension: namely, the extent to which foster placements end prematurely and the associated factors. This will be augmented by an analysis of casenotes in order to ascertain the extent to which social workers perceive that the aims of a placement have been met.

We do not feel that the research is unduly restricted by concentrating, in our extensive study, on the duration of placements. We saw in the opening chapter that placement instability in the child care system is a serious problem and it is important to make available up-to-date evidence on the rates of fostering breakdown. In addition, as with the problem of absconding from residential institutions, esoteric debates about how to meet children's needs more effectively are somewhat superfluous if, in the meantime, the child has departed. A more ambitious project would also have substantial resource implications and we are pleased to seek to clear some of the path for others to follow.

It is also important to consider carefully the language used to describe placement outcome and there is an elaborate nomenclature at our disposal. The most popular term in current usage for the premature ending of a foster placement is 'disruption'.[10] However, in contrast to established practice, we believe the term 'breakdown' is more appropriate. 'Disruption' is a euphemism. It is a nicety that suggests a temporary setback to a care plan and an unfortunate hiccup for the social worker. All our research, however, leads to different conclusions: from the child's point of view, unplanned changes in placement are often highly distressing, they lead to setbacks in schooling, a residential interlude often ensues and contacts with natural parents can become increasingly tenuous. An important conclusion of this study is that social workers often underestimate the effects of placement change – particularly on children but also on other participants, such as foster parents. Thus, we feel that 'breakdown' more accurately conveys the reality of the situation and, if the term was used more extensively, greater sensitivity might be evident in managing children's care careers.

In preferring the expression 'breakdown', however, we are not implying that there is necessarily anything final about the experience. Indeed, in scrutinizing the several hundred case histories, we were constantly impressed by children's resilience. Neither should the choice of the term be interpreted as suggesting that placements that break down are wholly negative. Rather like marriages, those turbulent experiences that soon expire can be richly rewarding; whereas those that stagger on can have long ceased to serve a useful function. Moreover, by focusing on the problem of breakdown, our study is not being unduly pessimistic: we also examine placements that endure in order to highlight the salient differences. Furthermore, in using the term 'breakdown' rather than the more emotionally neutral 'disruption', we do not intend to apportion blame for what happened to foster parents or to anyone else. Preference for a euphemistic term occurs essentially to assuage feelings of guilt; particularly on the part of foster parents. Whereas continued use of a euphemism may be justified in this latter context, the focus of our research is children and, therefore, we shall use the term which reflects the reality of their situation.

'Breakdown' has been defined and measured by various observers in a multitude of ways. The influential report of the Audit Commission on child care provision, for example, adopted an unusually broad categorization. It defined as a 'breakdown' any permanent move from a foster home – other than return to a child's natural family – which occurred more than three months after entry to care.[11] In contrast, our definition of 'breakdown' is as follows: 'A placement ending that was not included in the social work plan, either in the ending itself or the timing of the termination.'

As acknowledged earlier, an inescapable problem is that social workers' objectives are not always explicit (or clearly formulated) and, in the extensive survey, these had to be gleaned from casenotes, review and case conference documents, and special reports. In those few cases where no indication could be discovered, we interviewed the social worker responsible for the case.

Our conceptualization of placement breakdown has two further dimensions. First, we differentiate between breakdowns in 'crisis' circumstances and those which merely brought forward planned changes, as in the case of short-term fosterings. Indeed, in relation to short-term foster care, it is also interesting to consider whether a placement that lasts significantly *longer* than intended also signifies a form of 'breakdown' in the social work plan. Where this occurred, separate provision was made for its recording. A second distinction made in our classification of 'breakdowns' was to assess the relative significance of child-, family- and placement-related reasons for the termination. Clearly, many factors were interrelated but this categorization proved fruitful.

Methodology

With these theoretical and conceptual problems thus clarified, we shall now round off this chapter by describing some of the practical issues surrounding the research. It was decided to undertake the study in three contrasting social work agencies – two Social Services Departments and one voluntary child care organization. Gaining access to an agency for child care research entails, rightly, an elaborate and highly delicate series of negotiations which, in comparison, makes selling double-glazing seem second nature. After successive meetings with senior managers, middle managers, research officers, fostering personnel, team leaders and social workers, approval was granted and mutual responsibilities agreed. Though requiring considerable time and effort at the preparatory stage, these initial consultations were later to pay dividends: communication problems were less likely to occur and relationships with practitioners were stronger. The series of meetings also yielded useful insights into the functioning of the agencies and highlighted important, additional issues that could be incorporated in the research.

The two local authority departments selected for the research differed in their geography, administration and professional practice. Both had previously participated in the study of children's homes referred to in the opening chapter. Hence, detailed information concerning fostering could be located in a broader context of child care practice. One agency is part of a large, predominantly rural county in the South of England with a population approaching a million, most of whom live in an urban centre to the west of the county. The rate of children in care is similar to the national average (6.5 per thousand). Traditionally, the county has fostered a relatively high proportion of its children in care, approximately two-thirds. Fostering services in the county can be described as 'generic' rather than 'specialist'. Few personnel are employed with specific responsibility for foster care and, instead, social workers are heavily involved in recruiting, assessing and supporting family placements. The area of the county selected for study was covered by 12 social work teams. Throughout this study, we shall refer to this Social Services Department in the South of England as 'the County Authority'.

In contrast to this relative tranquillity, the second agency participating in the study is an inner London borough, with one of the highest levels of social and economic disadvantage in the United Kingdom. It has a population of some quarter of a million which, in common with many inner city areas, has declined noticeably in recent years, with a marked decrease among the under-fives. The borough has a large ethnic minority population, with a quarter of residents having been born abroad. The degree of disadvantage present in this area of London is apparent from some comparative statistics: it has the highest level of homelessness in London; the highest number of hospital admissions and readmissions concerning mental health; two-thirds of households in the borough claim Supplementary Benefit; and one family in three with dependent children is headed by a single parent. Not surprisingly, the rate of children in care in the borough is among the highest in the country, at three times the national average – approaching twenty per thousand children. The proportion of children in care accommodated in foster homes is lower than the national figure, and in the County Authority, at approximately 50 per cent.

The organization of child care services in this London borough is somewhat different than in the County Authority described earlier. Aided by its geographical concentration, management is centralized and services tend to be more 'specialist'. Thus, the fostering section of the Borough is a sizeable and impressive grouping and each of the eight areas into which social work services are sub-divided has a liaison fostering officer, who offers social workers specialist advice and is knowledgeable of local fostering resources. Following early negotiations in the borough, we approached four of the eight social work areas to seek their involvement in the research; each of which subsequently agreed. In subsequent chapters, we shall refer to this agency as 'the London Borough'.

It is important to mention one other feature of child care policy development in the London Borough. Since the early

1980s, efforts have been made to reduce the number of children living in long-term foster homes. Especially for children below the age of ten, more resources have been directed towards rehabilitation and, if this proves impracticable within a given period (usually a year), 'permanency' – in the form of adoption – is preferred. This policy has not been without its critics, both within as well as without the borough. Obviously, our research was unable to examine the outcome of such adoption placements. However, it would seem highly desirable for some evaluative research to be undertaken on this issue; particularly for placements involving older children, those for whom some form of attachment to natural parents had occurred prior to separation and cases in which the adoption was contested.

The third fostering service to be scrutinized in the research was a specialist scheme run by a major voluntary child care organization. This catered for children whom local authorities had found difficult to place. In the following chapters, this organization is referred to as 'the Voluntary Agency'. Obviously, owing to the labour-intensive nature of the investigation, we were unable to survey more widely the voluntary sector. However, as with our previous research, we felt it important to include one such scheme to provide at least a degree of comparison.

The scheme managed by the Voluntary Agency was located in the South-East of England and had been in operation five years. Referrals came from a broad range of local authorities, although the London boroughs predominated. The scheme catered for 'children with special needs': those with physical or mental handicaps; children exhibiting learning or behavioural problems; and sibling groups whom it was wished not to separate. Seven specialist social workers and additional support staff were employed. An interesting feature of the project was its use of residential care. Prior to family placement, each child accepted for the scheme lived for an average of eight or nine months in a residential facility, managed also by the Voluntary Agency. This served as a base for the introduction of a child to the family selected by the scheme. After a child has been placed with a family, intensive support is offered for the first six months by a project social worker and a residential 'key worker', who, throughout, has been closely involved with the child. Subsequently, the social worker from the child's own local authority will assume greater responsibility for the placement, although couples are encouraged to attend regular group support meetings, organized by the Voluntary Agency, for foster and adoptive parents.

A detailed schedue was designed on the basis of our early exploration of the literature on fostering breakdown, discussions with representatives from the three participating agencies and the research questions posed at the end of the previous chapter. This research instrument standardized the information gathered from social workers' records for our extensive, statistical survey. This schedule ran to 14 pages and included 58 questions recording both quantitative and qualitative data. Broad areas addressed by the schedule included: information to enable breakdown rates to be calculated, including aims of the placement and its duration; qualitative material, where applicable, on the effects of a breakdown on participants and subsequent management; and information pertaining to the three perspectives discussed in the opening section of this chapter, namely children's early rearing histories and care careers, their social networks and the characteristics of the foster household. Before fieldwork commenced, this schedule was piloted on 15 cases in one social work team in the County Authority and appropriate modifications were made.

In order to standardize the study samples in each social work team visited in the County Authority and the London Borough, a survey date was decided – 1 August 1983. Two study populations were then compiled. The first consisted of a 'long-stay' group: all children in care on the survey date who had been in care continuously for more than a year and who, at some stage during the current care period, had been fostered. The second study sample was a 'short-stay' group:

children who, in the twelve months prior to 1 August 1983, had both entered and left care, whose stay in care had thus been less than a year, and who had been fostered at some stage during this period. It is important to emphasize that, for both 'long' and 'short' stay samples, information was gathered (and a schedule completed) on *each* foster placement experienced by the child during the relevant care period. Furthermore, with the exception of short-term fosterings, only cases in which placements *could* have lasted at least a year (i.e., were made on or before August 1982) were surveyed. Otherwise, following our definition, such fosterings could not possibly have 'succeeded' – that is, endured for longer than a year – and the breakdown rate would have been distorted. Since the Voluntary Agency participating in the research did not, as such, admit children to 'care', arrangements were rather less complex and we examined the records of all children placed by the project with foster families prior to the relevant date.

Apart from regular and welcome diversions, during our visits to the 17 teams we were, thus, occupied in reading social workers' casenotes. In total, 372 children's files were carefully scrutinized: those of the 246 children in the 'long-stay' group, the 90 'short-stay' cases and the 36 children dealt with by the Voluntary Agency. Statistical information derived from the 'extensive' survey was stored and analysed on computer. Multivariate analysis was undertaken by using a technique known as 'Stepwise Logistic Progression'.[12]

Social workers' records ranged in magnitude from a few sheets of paper to one adolescent, in care since birth, whose file – running to several volumes – occupied the entire drawer of a filing cabinet and the best part of a day of the researchers' time. As one would expect, records varied in quality yet the exercise provided a fascinating insight into social work practice, priorities and anxieties. Significantly, whereas reams of material were usually recorded on children's casenotes, foster parents' records were much more sparse and relevant information was often difficult to discover.

Research in a social work team is a salutary experience. The County Authority participating in the research was, and still is, in the midst of profound administrative reorganization and it was not always easy to track down the office in which social work teams, and their irreplaceable casefiles, had been relocated. One building in which four of the teams were based was the former workhouse of the northern section of the city and our concern was aroused somewhat by men dressed in spacesuits perambulating the building, ripping strips of asbestos from corridors. Our fieldwork visit to one social work team occurred in the aftermath of the death of a child in its care, following return to its natural parents. The levels of stress and tension generated by that tragic episode – and its public dissection – were unimaginable and we are indebted to those directly and indirectly concerned for allowing us access to confidential material at such a delicate time.

The second phase of our research – the intensive study of a small number of placements in which breakdown occurred – was undertaken after the statistical survey in social work teams had been completed. We were, therefore, able to explore in detail in interviews insights obtained from a broad knowledge of fostering and social work practice. It was decided that the cases selected for intensive study should each be located in the County Authority. This was to some degree on the grounds of pragmatism – proximity and cost – but also, as we shall see, breakdown rates were significantly higher in the County Authority than in the London Borough and it seemed particularly important to explore the processes involved in greater detail. However, this was augmented in the London Borough by meetings with foster parents, organized by the local branch of the National Foster Care Association, which yielded valuable information on their situation.

After careful consideration and a balancing of the resource implications, we concluded that the optimum number of cases for intensive investigation was ten. Therefore, in consultation with a manager from the County Authority with responsibility for foster care, the most recent cases in which breakdown had resulted were selected. These were chosen to represent different types of foster care and comprised: three planned long-term fosterings; three intended short-stay placements; and four adolescents on either an 'intermediate' placement or a 'special fostering scheme'.

In all ten cases, we sought to interview, where appropriate, each participant who had been involved, namely: social workers; foster parents; foster children; natural parents; residential 'key workers', if involved prior, during or subsequent to placements; and finally – as the educational implications of social work decisions and practice are so frequently disregarded – a teacher of close acquaintance with the child. Initially, we contacted team leaders and social workers and, having been reassured that interviews would be conducted sensitively and confidentially, permission was obtained to proceed with each of the ten cases. In total, interviews were completed with; ten social workers, five social workers allocated to work with and support the foster households, seven natural parents, eight residential workers and seven teachers. In addition, more informal 'interviews' were held with seven children; the other three being too young. Only two interviews, both concerning natural mothers, were refused: one was contesting a particularly contentious Adoption Order and the other, after remarrying, had moved to the North of England following threatened violence to his stepfather from her teenage son.

Interviews were semi-structured and we pursued broad themes which had emerged as significant from the extensive survey. Resources available for the research allowed us to undertake only one interview with each participant but we carefully explored the progress of the fostering over time, ranging from participants' experiences and expectations before the placement was made to its development once the child had moved in. Particular attention was focused on the perspectives of participants and, especially, on the negotiations that occurred prior to the breakdown. All questions were open-ended, however, and respondents were encouraged to raise important issues that they felt we had overlooked.

The majority of interviews were tape-recorded, although all subjects were asked at the outset if they preferred otherwise in which case a written record was taken. Relevant sections of recordings were transcribed. In only three of the seven interviews with children – each were older adolescents – was it felt appropriate to use a tape-recorder.

Conclusion

In this chapter we have considered the following issues: the theoretical basis of the study; exactly what is meant by some of the more important terms that we employ; and the way in which the information was gathered.

Any research design must seek to balance pragmatism and efficacy and ours is no exception. We thus complement a broad statistical survey with a more intensive exploration of a small number of cases in which fostering breakdown occurred. In this way, the themes that are highlighted can be examined from a range of perspectives and the interactions between the parties involved can be explored. Conceptually, we also feel that it is necessary to differentiate carefully between different types of fostering and to keep these in mind when considering findings. Furthermore, by focusing attention on the notion of 'breakdown', we hope that the understanding of the following chapters is enhanced.

Finally, our description of the methodological approach adopted in the study reveals the range and amount of information that was gathered. It is a considerable challenge to summarize coherently such a store of data and, given the slightest opportunity, computers endlessly pour our interesting and significant results. Our months engaged in fieldwork yielded some fascinating insights into child care practice and we hope that, in the following chapters, we can do justice to this material and assist understanding of the problem of fostering breakdown.

Notes

1 J. Bowlby, *Maternal Care and Mental Health*, World Health Organisation Monograph Series No. 2, WHO, 1952.
2 See for example M. Rutter, *Maternal Deprivation Reassessed*, Penguin, 1974.
3 S. Millham, R. Bullock, K. Hosie and M. Haak, *Lost in Care: The Problems of Maintaining Links Between Children in Care and their Families*, Gower, 1986.
4 See for example M. Stein and K. Carey, *Leaving Care*, Basil Blackwell, 1986.
5 See B. Sutton Smith, *The Sibling*, Holt, Rinehart and Winston, 1970; W. Hartup, 'Peer interaction and social organisation' in P. Mussen ed., *Carmichael's Manual of Child Psychology*, vol. II, Wiley and Son, 1970; J. Bruner, M. Cole and B. Lloyd eds, *Children's Friendships: The Developing Child*, Fontana, 1980.
6 For example T. Luckmann ed., *Phenomenology and Sociology*, Penguin, 1978.
7 L. Lambert and J. Seglow, *Adoption Allowances: The Early Years of an Innovatory Scheme*, National Children's Bureau, 1987.
8 One interesting exception is B. Jassal, *Short-Term Foster Care*, National Foster Care Association, 1982.
9 See note to table 1.1 to chapter 1.
10 See for example J. Fitzgerald, *Understanding Disruption*, British Agencies for Adoption and Fostering, 1983; K. Donley, 'The dynamics of disruption', *Adoption and Fostering*, vol. 2, no. 2, 1978, pp. 34–9.
11 Department of the Environment, *The Provision of Child Care: A Study at Eight Local Authorities in England and Wales*, 1981.
12 See W. Dixon ed., *BMDP Statistical Software*, University of California Press, 1985.

3

Long-Term Foster Care:
Paul – a Case Study

We begin our analysis of findings from this study of fostering breakdown by focusing on planned long-term placements. In the following chapter, we consider some of the broader results from our extensive, statistical survey. First, however, we shall briefly introduce the case study of Paul Thornton, who was one of the three children experiencing an intended long-term foster placement featured in our intensive study. Obviously, each child's situation is unique but, as we shall see later, a number of themes evident in this case study apply more widely.

When visited at the children's home at which he was then living, Paul appeared as a withdrawn, softly-spoken child, who was both physically and emotionally immature for an 11-year old. Since his foster placement broke down, he had been living in residential care for four months. Indeed, apart from the interlude of twelve months spent with his foster family – the Gilbeys – Paul had been living at the children's home for the past five years.

The Thornton family have encountered problems over a long period. During the first six years of his life, Paul – together with his sister Maureen, who is three years his senior, and Geoff, who is two years older than Maureen – experienced several voluntary receptions into care. These occurred for a variety of reasons but there were certain recurring circumstances. Paul's mother suffered prolonged ill-health and was involved in prostitution, while the marital relationship was turbulent and Mr Thornton involved himself in a succession of highly complex and precarious relationships with other women. At the time of the interview Paul's brother, Geoff, was living with long-term foster parents, in what Paul's social worker – Judy Chambers – described as a situation of virtual adoption. Geoff had been separated from his siblings from an early age. His sister, in contrast, was believed to be living in a flat with friends. For whatever reason Geoff, Maureen and Paul each had different social workers.

When Paul was seven, he and his sister were again admitted to care and have not lived permenently at home since. Mr Thornton was deeply committed to a fresh affaire, while his wife's 'mode of life and habits', as the official report quaintly put it, was causing concern to the Social Services Department. Hence, Paul and Maureen were received into voluntary care, which was eventually followed by a parental rights resolution (Section 3, Child Care Act 1980). Efforts were made to place the children together in a foster home but this plan was soon abandoned once it was discovered that there was a dearth of foster families in the city who were prepared to accept sibling groups. Thus, Maureen was placed with foster parents on the border of the county, while it was decided to place Paul in St Mary's, a medium-size children's home near the city centre. This establishment, run by a Catholic Child Welfare Agency, enjoyed magnificent views across the city and, from a distance, would appear to those few residents in the inner city who were not dependent on social services – as a client or an employee – as either a conference centre or a luxury hotel. Its quality of child care was similarly impressive.

Paul's placement in the children's home was made for a variety of reasons. Initially, and to her credit, Paul's social worker at the time had made extensive investigations among Paul's wider family – spread over a considerable geographical area – to see whether there was a possibility that he could live with any of them and, thus, avoid being received into care. To everyone's consternation, and contrary to professional expectations, Paul settled reasonably comfortably in the children's home and the arrangement seemed to suit mother and son, who would see each other twice a week. This situation persisted for nine months: Mrs Thornton and Paul were convinced they were soon to be reunited, whereas their social worker was rather less enthusiastic and believed that a more rewarding and secure family life could be provided for Paul by foster parents. However, undue prognostication on the part of the social worker proved unnecessary, as she was soon to resign from her job in order to take up a senior post in an adjoining county.

The new social worker appointed to work with Paul was Judy Chambers. Her concern for Paul's future development was soon aroused, as she could see no likelihood of the situation being resolved unless she forced some of the issues – in particular, until she confronted Mrs Thornton about the way in which they could ensure a more permanent future for her son. Like her predecessor, Judy Chambers believed that Paul's best hope for security would be with a long-term foster family; these sentiments were also being strongly reinforced by colleagues who participated in reviews of the case. Thus, when Paul was seven and had been living at the children's home for a year, efforts were made to prepare Paul – and, perhaps more problematically, his mother – for a move to a foster family. Mrs Thornton, though initially resentful, was eventually persuaded and reassured that contact between her and her son could continue.

However, plans did not progress quite as smoothly as was envisaged. Paul was a young child and his behaviour was not particularly difficult and so, one would have thought, finding suitable foster parents should have been relatively straightforward. Yet it was no less than two-and-a-half years before an appropriate couple was located. Within the

County Authority, it will be recalled, individual social workers were responsible for finding long-term foster parents and no centralized system existed. As Judy Chambers explained:

I was flabbergasted – two and a half years it took! I couldn't believe it, it was a real eye-opener to me. 'Always prefer fostering to residential care' I was taught at college. Easier said than done. I must admit that looking at prospective foster parents was very time-consuming and I had the rest of my caseload to think of, of course, and it wasn't as if Paul was being disruptive at St Mary's, was it? They must have thought I was sitting on my backside. At case reviews my team leader kept looking at the past forms and saying 'Why isn't he in a foster home yet?' I used to dread those meetings. I told him if he was so clever, he could go out and find me one. The other problem at the time was that our car travel allowance had been cut and we were only supposed to do so many miles a month. I was way over most months and would usually get a rollocking for that as well. That's local government for you! No, I learned a lot from that experience and I approach fostering a bit different now than I used to.

Over the two-and-a-half year period spent searching for foster parents, Judy Chambers reported that she discovered only seven families that she could seriously consider. In desperation, she also advertised in the local press – receiving only three responses – 'Two were totally unsuitable and there was one complete weirdo'. However, after this thorough combing of the area, a suitable family – the Gilbeys – did eventually present itself, having recently moved from the North of England because of Mr Gilbey's work with a firm that specialized in computer software. After careful consideration, Miss Chambers was convinced that the Gilbeys were a suitable family for Paul. She reported that Paul, who was by now in his last year of primary school, was also relieved as, while living in his children's home, he had been surrounded by other children being prepared for, and moving on to, foster homes and by others returning after their fosterings had failed.

Paul's foster placement

For Mr and Mrs Gilbey, this was to be their first experience of fostering, although Mrs Gilbey had been a childminder prior to moving. When interviewed, they obviously seemed a warm and intelligent couple, rather middle-class, who were aspirant in terms of social status and proud of their large, renovated house in a desirable part of the city. Mr and Mrs Gilbey also had two daughters of their own – aged nine and six – and one of their reasons for fostering, they revealed, was that they felt their family would be more complete with a boy. It was also thought that the girls would like a brother of a similar age.

From the date of their application to the Social Services Department to become foster parents, which arose from seeing an item on local television, it was six months before they were finally 'approved' as long-term foster parents and informed that a possible child for them – Paul – had been found. Mr Gilbey commented: 'The Social Services wrote to us and said that we had now been "vetted". I always thought that "vetting" was what you did when you had cats neutered.'

During the six month wait, the Gilbeys had attended foster parent training sessions, met other foster parents and they were generally impressed with the preparation they had received. The initial meeting between Paul and Mr and Mrs Gilbey occurred at St Mary's children's home in January. Contact was gradually increased, until Paul was spending every weekend with his foster family and the intention was for Paul to move in July, so that he would – hopefully – be settled in his new home prior to transferring to the comprehensive school in the autumn. As planned, the move materialized in July. When questioned, the foster parents felt that, in retrospect, the introduction stage had been handled sensitively and that the timing was about right.

Initially, Mr and Mrs Gilbey felt that Paul had settled in with them very well – in fact, too well – and they awaited the completion of the 'honeymoon period', about which they had been warned at their preparatory meetings. After about a month, changes in Paul's behaviour duly occurred, as it became apparent to Mr and Mrs Gilbey that they were fostering an extremely insecure child. His behaviour became very attention-seeking; he would frequently disrupt the two sisters when he felt that he was being ignored; and, whenever other adults visited the household, Paul would constantly cling to them. This last trait of Paul was also a feature of his relationship with his foster mother and he was reported to have followed her everywhere she went throughout the house. As Mrs Gilbey remarked:

I just couldn't get away from him when he was home from school, it made me want to scream. I know he wanted a lot of personal attention and we were prepared for that but I felt just as if he was suffocating me. It even got to the stage that he would follow me to the loo and wait for me outside until I had finished!

Thus, difficulties were evident from an early stage in the placement and Paul also began to misbehave in an irritating manner. One aspect of the experience that puzzled Mr and Mrs Gilbey was that they saw very little of Paul's social worker in the first few weeks. Judy Chambers explained the reasoning behind this when interviewed: 'I tend to stay away to begin with and let the placement "settle". I don't think that foster parents always want to be pestered by social workers popping in and out and it gives time for things to get established. No, I think it's best to keep a low profile at the start.'

It is important to note that the social worker's perceptions were not confirmed by Mr and Mrs Gilbey, who commented that greater outside involvement would have been welcomed. Mrs Gilbey, for example, remarked:

We thought we'd done something to upset her – I phoned her up and asked what was wrong. She told us later why she had deliberately kept out of it and I told her then I didn't agree with it. It was the first time we'd fostered and we felt so alone at the start. All our friends stayed away and even our two got a bit distant. Not surprising when you think of what hit us.

Schooling

Paul's education, which was now the responsibility of his new, much larger and rather more impersonal comprehensive school, was also not without its problems. Mrs Andrews, his first year form tutor, reported that Paul was believed to be of average ability but was certainly underachieving. His progress has since improved markedly, but his transfer to the new school was an extremely testing time for all. Paul was said to be disruptive in class, while he made and terminated friendships with remarkable alacrity. Mrs Andrews was aware from the outset that Paul lived with foster parents. She met Mr and Mrs Gilbey at parents' functions but had never been introduced to Paul's social worker. She also felt that the absence of any detailed information on his educational and social background was a distinct disadvantage in trying effectively to plan Paul's schooling.

There is a further, somewhat bizarre, element to Paul's educational experience. In the January of his second term at the comprehensive school, Paul's head teacher observed that there was a senior pupil in the final year of the school who was also named Thornton – and that, in appearance, the two boys were not dissimilar. One morning, the headmaster – with a certain degree of sensitivity and foresight – asked Paul whether he had an older brother. Paul replied that he had an older sister, Maureen, but thought he did not have an older brother. He would, however, check with his social worker. The degree of uncertainty reflects the effort invested in assisting Paul to understand and come to terms with his past. On her next visit to the household, Paul broached the subject with Judy Chambers. She informed him that he did, indeed, have an older brother, who had been separated from his family at a very early age. She also took the opportunity – somewhat belatedly, one might feel – to raise with Paul other features of his upbringing. At the first opportunity, Paul conveyed this news to his headteacher and, as chance would have it, it transpired that the senior pupil was no other than Paul's brother Geoff: a situation worthy of the concluding chapter of a Dickens novel. Geoff's social worker occupied the office adjacent to Judy Chambers and this unfortunate episode reveals the degree of communication between the two about the Thornton family.

The effects of this disclosure on Paul were mixed. Initially, both he and Geoff were pleasantly surprised to discover that they each had a long-lost brother and it would seem that a mutually rewarding relationship developed between the two. In contrast, however, this remarkable act of fate soon reverberated throughout the school and became a popular topic of discussion. Geoff, being a sizeable skinhead, who was given a wide berth by most teachers – let alone pupils – in the school, could more than adequately look after himself. Paul, on the other hand, soon became an object of derision among his peers, when it was more widely discovered that he was living with foster parents and was unaware of the membership of his own family. Although the indignity and humiliation eventually subsided, the mark that was left on Paul's schooling – and, in particular, the way in which this exacerbated the problems associated with transfer to the new school – should not be underestimated.

In addition, difficulties persisted at the foster home and it was in April – nine months after he arrived – that the Social Services Department became aware that the placement was rapidly deteriorating. Paul continued to shadow Mrs Gilbey wherever she went and the latter was spending more and more time in activities outside the home, such as Girl Guides and other functions associated with the church. This caused concern to Judy Chambers, who suspected something was amiss.

There were also problems surrounding Paul's contact with his natural parents. Mr Thornton, still entrenched in his new liaison, expressed little interest in his son. The situation of Mrs Thornton was rather different. Paul's foster parents and Mrs Thornton had never met. For reasons that are not completely clear, Mrs Thornton had never been allowed to visit Paul at his foster home. She did not even know their address. Consequently, Paul would meet his mother once a week at St Mary's children's home; an arrangement which the head of the home, Sister Jeanette, considered far from satisfactory. In interview, Judy Chambers admitted that these access arrangements did not fully meet Paul's needs but that she felt they were necessary to placate the foster parents and, thereby, not jeopardize the placement. Mr and Mrs Gilbey, however, did not corroborate this view.

Other conflicts arose in the foster home. Despite their continual efforts, Paul refused to call his foster parents 'mum' and 'dad'. There were also problems in the relationship with the Gilbeys' daughters. Considerable jealousy had surfaced between the three children; Mr and Mrs Gilbey felt that their own daughters were being neglected as they had to dedicate so much of themselves to Paul; and there was concern that Paul might, on some future occasion, act violently towards the girls.

The fostering breaks down

For these reasons, and a multitude of others, Mr and Mrs Gilbey reluctantly decided that, after a stay of a year with their family, Paul would have to go. On being requested to visit the Gilbeys, Judy Chambers was completely taken aback when informed of this decision and her plea for the foster parents to reconsider was rejected.

Following the breakdown, Paul returned to St Mary's children's home, where an informal 'interview' was arranged with him. However, not unexpectedly, he was unwilling or unable to articulate his thoughts about his experience, apart from saying that he liked living with Mr and Mrs Gilbey, he missed their dog (not their daughters, interestingly) and was sorry that he had to leave them. Nevertheless, he continues to refer to the couple as 'my foster parents' and, significantly, contact with them has been maintained.

Paul's key worker at St Mary's – Joyce – was able to provide more insight into his adjustment since the foster placement ended. She had known Paul prior to his moving to the Gilbeys and, thus, was well qualified to comment. On returning to St Mary's, Paul was said to be extremely subdued. He had returned to the same environment and to most of the same staff but Paul knew few children and he found it difficult to build up new friendships. Paul said little about his fostering experience. Joyce felt, however, that his fragile self-confidence had received a tremendous setback. This was exacerbated by the way in which the placement ended. Paul, rather like his social worker, had not anticipated his removal and was unprepared for it. His foster parents had assumed that both Paul and his social worker realized that the placement was deteriorating and that his removal was a possibility. Judy Chambers observed that events on the morning that she returned Paul to St Mary's symbolized other aspects of the placement:

Well, I went to collect Paul that morning and I hate having to do it because everybody always gets upset and emotional. But I had planned to help Paul pack his things so that we could spend some time together and I could help him (and me) to come to terms with the fact that he had suffered a rejection. When I arrived there, though, the Gilbeys had already packed all his toys and clothes in some carrier bags and they were all lined up in the hall. Mrs Gilbey let me in – she couldn't speak to me she was that upset – and Paul was sitting on his own on the bottom of the stairs and it hit me there and then just what a sad, lost little boy he is.

Paul's subsequent recuperation at St Mary's was hindered by two further setbacks. First, the head of the children's home – Sister Jeanette – a warm, effervescent and charismatic figure, was instructed by her religious Order that she was to move to a post elsewhere. Paul had been very close to the Sister and she was an important source of continuity in his life. Even more significantly, however, following an unsuccessful struggle for three years against cancer, Paul's mother died. He had become aware that his mother was terminally ill some months prior to her death, yet the effect on him was no less shattering. The day following her death, Paul arrived unexpectedly on Mrs Gilbey's doorstep. For the first time, she remarked, Paul burst into tears and poured out his feelings to her. In a memorable phrase, Mrs Gilbey described Paul as being 'a bottomless pit of despair'.

In a highly emotional interview, like many others involving foster parents, Mr and Mrs Gilbey retraced their experiences with Paul. They touched on many important issues but one recurring topic was the considerable impact that Paul, and his departure, had on the entire family. Fostering had placed great strains on family relationships, particularly between husband and wife. Mr Gilbey had felt for some months that the placement was in jeopardy, although his wife refused to accept this view. She had been transformed, according to her husband, into a different person and was totally manipulated by Paul. Similarly, the Gilbey's two daughters were felt to be adversely affected by the experience and relationships between them and their parents are now distinctly cool. The older girl, in particular, remains bitter with her parents for accepting a foster child into the household and her parents fear that Paul's presence will have had a lasting effect on her.

In facing the difficulties posed by Paul, Mr and Mrs Gilbey felt that they were very much left on their own to cope with the pressures of fostering. As newcomers to the experience, they found this astounding. Their most valuable source of support, they insisted, came from Sister Jeanette at the children's home and Mrs. Gilbey would often drop in to visit her when she was in town shopping. The contribution of Paul's social worker, on the other hand, was perceived as less useful. She would visit about once every three months and the foster parents sensed that she would deliberately keep at a distance if things were going well. Judy Chambers tacitly agreed with this last point and added that the last thing she wanted to do was 'rock the boat'. Some assistance in bailing out water, however, may have been useful. In any case, Mrs Gilbey felt that she could not admit defeat to the Social Services Department and, if she did, feared that she would never be allowed to foster again.

Moreover, Mr and Mrs Gilbey felt that, in retrospect, the placement had not had the best of beginnings. From the first time they met Paul in St Mary's, they felt that they were under considerable pressure to accept Paul into their family; indeed, they described this as a moral obligation which was virtually impossible to refuse. They were also given minimal background information on Paul and were, therefore, disadvantaged in discussing his early experiences with him ('He could have been telling us a pack of lies for all we knew'). The Gilbeys were inflicted with a sense of failure and profound guilt. Despite the sensitive way in which Judy Chambers had subsequently helped them and insisted that, with this learning experience behind them, they would go on to make excellent foster parents, Mr and Mrs Gilbey feel that they – and their daughters – have made a sufficient sacrifice and would not wish to risk a repetition.

Finally, Judy Chambers offered some general observations on the experience from the social work perspective. Clearly, this was not an easy case to handle and Mrs Thornton's recent death posed additional problems. Nevertheless, the social worker was now able to view matters more objectively than when she was preoccupied with simply maintaining the placement. For example she admitted that, from the outset, she had reservations about whether the Gilbeys were completely appropriate for Paul: they were inexperienced foster parents, they seemed to her rather too middle-class, fuelled by a sense of social duty, and their expectations of Paul could be unrealistic. If these problems had been confronted, the social worker would have envisaged enormous difficulties and so 'I just stayed away and kept hoping'. She also added that parental contact was kept to a minimum 'so as to try to keep the placement going'. As she agreed, however, this plan may have served a purpose in the short-term (and as the situation developed, it did not even do this), yet it would do little to promote Paul's long-term interests. Despite these reservations, after searching for over two years, Miss Chambers was under pressure from her senior colleagues to move Paul out of residential care and into a foster home. She remarked, 'With hindsight, I should have resisted and followed my own instincts'.

It also transpired that the social worker found her visits to the foster household extremely stressful. Indeed, one appreciates why *natural parents*, even when invited, prefer to stay away. She sensed that her visits to the Gilbeys were unwelcome and she felt that she was intruding. Yet, as we have noted earlier, the foster parents themselves did not reinforce this view. Furthermore, the educational arrangements – whereby Paul and Geoff were attending the same school – were admitted to have been handled disastrously. Although she feels that she and her colleague were 'unlucky', she concurred that the situation should have been handled differently.

As the fostering breakdown was unexpected, at the time of interview future plans for Paul were unclear and were complicated by the need to help him to cope following his mother's death. In the immediate future, Judy Chambers was convinced that Paul would be unable to respond to another fostering experience and, in many respects, the most suitable intermediate measure would have been a small 'family group' children's home. None of these, however, existed in Paul's division of the county. Perhaps surprisingly, another option that was being seriously considered was whether Paul might return to live with his father. His social worker added, however, that this arrangement would require considerable work on her part. Nevertheless, Mr Thornton was then cohabiting in a steady relationship, he was in regular employment as a taxi driver and his drinking appeared to be under control. Judy Chambers confirmed, however, that this possibility had arisen out of default rather than design.

Conclusion

From this brief case study, we can observe several factors common to unsuccessful foster placements. We shall expand on these throughout the book but, at this stage, it may be helpful to identify them. For example, we saw the difficulty of matching Paul with appropriate foster parents. The social worker was under pressure from her Department to find a family placement for Paul and, in retrospect, admits that she should have been more critical in her assessment. It is also significant that it was the Gilbeys' first experience of fostering and, with the benefit of hindsight, they feel that they were rather naive in not demanding more information about Paul and expressing their reservations about the placement. Clearly, as they freely admit, they were unaware what they were letting themselves in for.

Also evident are the effects of the fostering on Paul's social networks. Contacts with his natural parents were tenuous and their relationship with Paul's foster parents was virtually non-existent. Until fortuitously reunited with his brother, admission to care also led to the separation of Paul from his siblings. Moreover, problems in the foster household were compounded by the difficulties associated with transfer to the new comprehensive school and Paul's largely unsuccessful attempts to establish himself with his peers.

Another important theme underlying the case history concerns the impact on the dynamics of the Gilbey household. Paul's removal was not precipitated by major episodes of upheaval, such as acts of violence or running away. Instead, his influence was both more subtle and pervasive and the traditional pattern of family life gradually disintegrated. A rift developed between foster parents and conflicts ensued with their own daughters.

In addition, it is obvious that the effects of the breakdown on those directly concerned are profound. Though well used to disguising his feelings, Paul was clearly adversely affected by the move. Similarly, his foster parents experienced a deep sense of guilt and discontinued their involvement with the Social Services Department. Throughout this unfortunate experience, the isolation and lack of support for Mr and Mrs Gilbey and their family is evident. Finally we can observe the contribution of residential care prior, during and subsequent to the fostering. Let us now see to what extent these factors apply to long-term fostering more generally.

4

Long-Term Fostering

We begin our analysis of the extensive component of the study, which is based on a scrutiny of social workers' casenotes in the County Authority and the London Borough, by focusing on the problem of breakdown in planned long-term fostering. It will be recalled that the population selected for this part of the research consisted of children in care on the survey date (1 August, 1983) who, at that time, had been the statutory responsibility of the Social Services Department, continuously, for over a year. One of these was Paul, whom we met in the previous chapter. (The specialist scheme managed by the Voluntary Agency is considered in a later chapter.)

An important finding to emphasize at the outset concerns the significance of long-term fostering. Alongside the more specialist types of supplementary family care that are developing, it is clear from our study that planned long-term placements continued to fulfil an important role. Indeed, in the two study agencies, half of all foster placements experienced by our population of children (both long- and short-stay samples) were intended to be of the long-term variety and short-term fosterings accounted for the majority of the remainder. As we shall see, however, there were noticeable differences between the County Authority and the London

Borough. Nevertheless, the significance of new initiatives should not be overestimated and traditional, long-term fostering – despite its many drawbacks – is by no means yet redundant.

Breakdown rates

In this chapter, we shall merge together, rather than analyse separately, the contrasting situations of the two participating agencies in order to try to arrive at a broader understanding of fostering practice. Initially, however, it is interesting to compare the breakdown rates of the County Authority and the London Borough. In the opening chapter, we saw that studies of long-term fostering have consistently discovered breakdown rates of approximately 50 per cent, over periods ranging from two to five years. Comparative statistics for our two agencies, based on the definition of 'breakdown' provided in the previous chapter, are shown in table 4.1.

Clearly, there are marked differences between the two agencies, both in the levels of use and the success of long-term fostering. From the final two lines of the table we can see that placements broke down more than twice as frequently in the County Authority than in the London Borough. In the former, for example, 40 per cent of planned long-stay placements ended within three years, compared with only 15 per cent in the London Borough. Alternatively, if one adopts a five year time-span, the level of placement breakdown in the County Authority rose to virtually half. This finding suggests that, in this particular agency, little improvement has been made on the situation discovered by the disconcerting 1960s studies discussed in chapter 1.

Multivariate statistical analysis was used to examine whether differences in breakdown rates in long-term fostering between the County Authority and the London Borough can be attributed to contrasting child populations or whether dissimilarities in policy and practice are import-ant.[1] Detailed analysis revealed that variations in outcome

TABLE 4.1 BREAKDOWN RATES IN LONG-TERM FOSTERING

Type of fostering	Breakdown within 1 year (%)	Numbers placed[a]	Breakdown within 3 years (%)	Numbers placed	Breakdown within 5 years (%)	Numbers placed
Fostered with 'strangers'						
County Authority	20	181	42	155	48	122
London Borough	10	42	21	33	29	28
Fostered with relatives						
County Authority	11	9	0	6	0	4
London Borough	6	16	0	14	0	12
All long-term fostering						
County Authority	19	190	40	161	46	126
London Borough	9	58	15	47	20	40

[a] Placements are included only if they could have lasted the entire period.

are accounted for by variables that we consider in the following pages. Thus, for comparable groups of foster children and in the context of other findings to be presented, our results indicate, interestingly, that the more specialist approach adopted by the London Borough did not, in itself, appear to have a noticeable impact on long-term fostering outcomes. We return to this issue at the end of the chapter.

It is also evident from table 4.1 that at least part of the difference in long-term breakdown rates between the two agencies can be accounted for by the greater use of fostering with relatives in the London Borough. Within the 'three year' category, for example, 30 per cent of children in the London Borough were placed with relatives, compared with barely four per cent in the County Authority. The greater success, in terms of endurance, of fostering with relatives is demonstrated by the fact that no placements in the 'three' and 'five year' categories broke down, as did only two out of 25 in the 'one year' group.

These findings make even more puzzling the fact that, as demonstrated by national statistics presented in chapter 1, fostering with relatives would seem to be in decline.[2] However, this change may be more administrative than real and children living with relatives are now more likely to be supported financially in other ways or subsumed under a different category, rather than be admitted to care. Our case study, Paul Thornton, would not have been received into care if his social worker could have found relatives who were prepared to look after him. It will be interesting to observe, for example, whether current research into children in care but deemed 'home on trial' reveals an overlap between the two groups.[3] Children fostered with relatives are, clearly, in a quite different situation from those of their peers fostered with 'strangers': indeed, according to DHSS child care statistics, a significant proportion, approximately a third, were living in the same household prior to their change in legal status.[4] Thus, as with other studies, we shall concentrate in the remainder of this study on children fostered with non-relatives.

In order to standardize the presentation of material and, hopefully, avoid confusion, we shall also restrict the illustration of our discussion to statistics derived from a 'three year' definition of breakdown. Nonetheless, it is important to point out that findings in our investigation obtained from different time-scales were remarkably consistent.

Before moving on from this discussion of breakdown rates, it is necessary to ask whether there are now fewer long-term fostering breakdowns than there were previously. This view was expressed by managers in each of the participating agencies although, interestingly, social workers were rather less optimistic. As one social worker in the County Authority commented when interviewed:

I shouldn't think we're any more successful now then we ever were. Fostering's always a big gamble and a huge leap in the dark and it just depends if you're prepared to take the risk. The trouble is, we're under a lot of pressure here to try to keep to a minimum the number of children in residential homes. No, I'd be very surprised if you found that we're any better at fostering now than we used to be.

Our findings would support her scepticism. For example, if one divides long-term placements in the two agencies into two equal groups – and, thereby, 1978 becomes the median year – it transpires that breakdown rates for each group are virtually identical: 38 per cent of placements made before 1978 broke down compared to 39 per cent of those thereafter. It should be added that different types of children are now being fostered; although, conversely, specialist schemes for problematic children have become more abundant. Nevertheless, it must be concluded that we have no statistical evidence from our two agencies to support the view that long-term fostering breakdowns are now a more remote occurrence. Our scrutiny of several hundred fostering histories suggests that advances are more modest than is sometimes assumed.

Circumstances in which breakdowns occur

Having seen that placement breakdown is by no means uncommon – certainly in the County Authority – it is logical then to explore the circumstances in which so many fosterings end prematurely. Our intensive study provides us with the opportunity to explore this in detail. Indeed, Paul's experience gave some insight into these problems. At this stage, however, we shall try to present a more general view from our study of social workers' casenotes.

Readers will recall from chapter 1 that previous research has consistently demonstrated that, as with Paul Thornton and Mr and Mrs Gilbey, foster placements that break down tend to do so early on. Findings from our 'extensive' survey support this view. Of all planned long-term placements that eventually broke down, 40 per cent were terminated during the first year; half of these occurring within the first three months. A further 20 per cent of breakdowns took place within the second year. These findings reveal the vulnerability of fosterings in their early stages and suggest that, as in the case of Paul, problems soon become apparent – to the foster parents if not the social worker. The importance of adequate supervision early on for foster parents, foster children and, indeed, social workers is obvious from these results. In contrast, as we saw with our case study, there is often a tendency for social workers, to remain at a distance early on in order to let a placement 'settle'. From our results, this practice would appear to be counter-productive. There is also recent research evidence, confirmed in studies of divorce, to indicate that long-term visiting patterns are established in the first few weeks.[5] This reinforces the importance of early efforts. Furthermore, we shall see later in this chapter that the average period of introduction for children to new, long-term foster homes was, perhaps surprisingly, only a month. It is pertinent to ask whether a more carefully phased beginning might be expected to reveal problems that often so rapidly ensue.

Our investigation of records clearly indicated that breakdowns in long-term fostering cause considerable disruption, not only to children's lives but also to social workers' intentions. Contingency plans should breakdown occur were seldom constructed from the outset of a fostering; hence, keeping the placement going tended to be the primary objective. This was evident from our case study. Thus, of the 72 long-term placements that broke down within three years, in only seven did the terminations lead to the bringing forward of longer-term plans. In the remainder, social workers were forced to react to an unanticipated crisis and to construct an alternative placement rapidly. Indeed, as with Paul, three-quarters of all children experiencing breakdown of a long-term fostering were placed subsequently in a residential setting (50 per cent in an 'ordinary' children's home), reaffirming the continuing significance of residence and its interrelation with fostering.[6] In contrast, a fifth of children were transferred directly to other foster placements, while the finding that only two per cent immediately returned to parents or other relatives clearly demonstrates that fostering breakdowns did not lead to the reuniting of families. As we shall see, if anything, children were further distanced from their families – physically as well as psychologically – by the process of breakdown of a long-term foster placement.

Our concern with the problems of placement instability should not conceal the fact that the majority of placements do *not* break down and, even for those that do, benefits for the child will often accrue. Following the breakdown of his placement, for example, Paul maintained contact with his former foster parents – despite his social worker's ambivalence – and they remain important figures in his life. From our detailed examination of case records, we sought to establish social workers' overall perceptions of the extent to which long-term fosterings were meeting expectations. Results are set out in table 4.2.

TABLE 4.2 SOCIAL WORKERS' PERCEPTIONS OF LONG-TERM FOSTER PLACEMENTS[7]

Rating	Placements that did not break down (%)	Placements that broke down (%)	All placements (%)
Highly satisfactory	34	6	23
Generally satisfactory	43	36	40
Both satisfactory and unsatisfactory	13	42	24
Generally unsatisfactory	3	11	6
Highly unsatisfactory	6	3	5
No information	1	2	2

We can see from the table that social workers were convinced that the majority of long-term foster placements were meeting their aims. From their written notes, we ascertained that almost a quarter of all placements were perceived as 'highly satisfactory' and a further two-fifths as 'generally satisfactory'. In contrast, only one placement in nine aroused serious concern on the part of the social worker, while responses to a quarter were mixed. It is also noticeable that there is a statistically significant relationship between social workers' estimation of foster placements and subsequent outcome. It would be wrong, however, to deduce from this that social workers are always fully cognizant of the progress of a foster placement. As in the case of Paul Thornton, overseeing and supporting a foster family is a difficult – and perhaps inherently contradictory – role to negotiate; particularly as the social worker does not witness day to day interactions and family problems. Hence, social workers featuring in our research – including those whom we personally interviewed – often claimed to be excluded from foster placements and to feel superfluous. The following extract from a social worker's notes typifies this relationship:

I visited John today at his foster parents and the situation doesn't get any easier. I keep telling the Reynolds that I'm there to help them with any problems but I can tell they don't trust me and would rather I kept away. They always make me feel as if I'm checking up on them. Is it worth the effort? (Social worker, London Borough)

These findings are confirmed from our scrutiny of casenotes, review reports and special documents. In a third of planned long-term fosterings which ended prematurely, social workers' records revealed that there was a *strong* indication that the placement might break down. In a further two-fifths of cases, *some* indication of the impending breakdown was disclosed. However, in a significant minority of cases – 29 per cent – casenotes contained *no* hint whatsoever of the seriousness of the problem but, instead, satisfactory progress was recorded. Thus, when the crisis of breakdown eventually occurred, social workers were taken unawares and plans for the child's future had to be completely rethought. Clearly, this degree of incongruity hinders effective planning for children's futures.

Reasons for breakdown

Of particular interest were the reasons for long-term fostering breakdowns, and here we should re-emphasize that social workers' accounts inevitably reflected only one perspective. Nevertheless, our exploration of casenotes revealed some interesting findings, which could be explored more fully in interviews with a broader range of participants. Obviously, as we saw with our case study, reasons for breakdown are complex and we would expect a number of factors to be involved. Nonetheless, from a detailed analysis of social workers' accounts – and when breakdowns occurred, detailed reports were usually compiled – we sought to ascertain whether the reasons for breakdown were *primarily* what we termed child-, placement- or parent-focused or a combination of these three. Results are tabulated in table 4.3.

TABLE 4.3 REASONS GIVEN IN SOCIAL WORKERS' RECORDS FOR LONG-TERM FOSTERING BREAKDOWNS

Type of reason	(%)[a]
Child-focused	20
Natural parent-focused	1
Placement-focused	30
Child + parent-focused	1
Child + placement-focused	37
Parent + placement-focused	3
Child-, parent- + placement-focused	3
Other	4

[a] Number of cases studied, 72. As with other tables in this study where rounding has also occurred, percentage figures may not total 100.

As one might expect, the problems posed by foster children – either in isolation or in combination with other factors – played an important part in the demise of many long-term placements. The tolerance and resilience of many foster parents was quite remarkable and file after file listed the behavioural problems posed by children: aggressive outbursts, sullen withdrawal, prolonged enuresis or encopresis, petty delinquency, extreme instances of attention-seeking and rejection, and so on. Many foster parents – as with Mr and Mrs Gilbey, who looked after Paul Thornton – were clearly unprepared for the sorts of demands that severely emotionally deprived children would make on them. The expectation on the part of social work agencies that to experience 'ordinary' family life with foster parents would resolve the quite major problems that some children in our sample had previously presented was somewhat unrealistic, if not irresponsible; and both foster children and numerous foster parents suffered the consequences. One social worker that we interviewed expressed this in the following way:

I suppose because we're used to dealing with difficult kids we sometimes forget just how difficult they are and how hard ordinary families find it to cope. Looking back, I realize that I expected too much from these foster parents but I hoped that once Wayne had been with them for a while he would begin to sort himself out. I was wrong.

It is also interesting to observe from table 4.3 that the natural parents – and, indeed, wider families – of foster children had little direct influence on the deterioration of placements. This was demonstrated with Mrs Thornton whom, as we saw, never even met her son's foster parents. As other studies have shown, most natural parents have minimal involvement in the placements of children in care. We would fully concur with the conclusion of Rowe and her collleagues that, despite certain developments, most long-term fostering remains essentially traditional and 'exclusive', and social workers' as well as natural family involvement remains problematic.[8]

However, a particularly interesting finding revealed in table 4.3 – supporting one of our original hypotheses – concerns the significance of what can be termed 'placement-focused' reasons for breakdown: these are factors that emanate primarily from the foster household. We do not suggest that fostering is unproblematic; indeed, there can be few pursuits – including residential child care work – that are more taxing. Nevertheless, it was clear that in a small but not insignificant core of planned long-term placements, the problems posed by children were not insurmountable and, other things being equal, it did not seem unreasonable that a period of stability could have been expected. Obviously, the responsibility for inappropriate placements lies essentially with the agency and social workers responsible for recruitment and preparation. Our research unequivocally demonstrated that the selection of appropriate foster placements is a somewhat haphazard process. Indeed one, admittedly exceptional, example was of a social worker who, when 'vetting' foster parents, always furtively checked whether they rinsed out milk bottles as this – it was believed – was a strong indicator of a caring, home-loving couple!

'Placement-focused' reasons for breakdown, as one might expect, were extremely varied. However, in our long-term sample from the two agencies, of the 22 placements that were discontinued essentially for this reason, we have selected four at random in order to provide some idea of the range of circumstances that prevailed:

Girl (aged 7) Foster mother became pregnant, began rejecting the foster child and eventually insisted on her removal.

Boy (12) Foster parents decided to move to Scotland. Child had occasional contact with his natural father and refused to move away from his city of origin and friends.

Boy (11) Constant disagreements occurred betweeen foster parents and professionals involved in the case – particularly social workers and educational psychologists. The boy was eventually removed after foster parents refused to allow him to attend a day special school.

Girl (4) Foster mother received in-patient treatment for depression, having this girl, another foster child and three of her own children, each of whom was under the age of five.

These brief sketches provide some illustration of placement-related factors associated with the breakdown of long-term foster placements in our sample. Fostering demanding children is undoubtedly a complex venture. Identification and recruitment of households with the special attributes for looking after other people's children is also fraught with difficulty, while supporting placements poses problems for social workers. Despite these complexities, it is somewhat disquieting to discover that, in a significant proportion of long-term fostering breakdowns, neither children nor their families were posing serious problems to the stability of the placement.

Factors associated with long-term fostering breakdown

Having explored some of the reasons for breakdown in
long-term fostering, we shall now investigate more fully the
factors associated with breakdown by contrasting the 117
placements that lasted three years with the 72 that ended
prematurely. Our analysis will be organized around the
three perspectives introduced in chapter 2: characteristics,
early rearing histories and care experiences of children;
children's social networks; and, finally, a further exploration
of a variety of placement-related factors.

Characteristics, early rearing histories and care experiences of children

Boys outnumbered girls in our sample of long-term fosterings by three to two. Interestingly, however, there was no
overall difference in breakdown rates between the sexes.
Some observers may assume boys to be more problematic
than girls and, therefore, breakdown rates for the former to
be higher than the latter. This view would undoubtedly be
challenged by those, such as residential workers or teachers,
who have worked with girls – especially adolescents. Very
little is known about the specific circumstances and problems
of adolescent girls in care and further research into this area
could prove fruitful.[9]

Only twenty-three members of our study population, all
in the care of the London Borough, originated from black
or mixed-race families, although virtually all children were
born in England. Overall, the breakdown rate for long-
term fostering was lower for ethnic minority than white
children, although within the London Borough, placement
stability was similar regardless of racial origin of children.
Multivariate analysis confirmed that, independently of
other variables, ethnicity was not strongly related to
outcome.

Of particular concern to the London Borough, as with

many other urban departments, was the issue of transracial placements. The use of traditional long-term fostering, as we have seen, was declining in the London Borough; hence numbers are insufficient for comparative purposes. In addition, until relatively recently, relatively few black foster parents were forthcoming. Consequently, our findings on outcome according to the racial origins of children and foster parents are inconclusive and more detailed investigation of the subject would be warranted. Nevertheless, from our evidence and using our definition of outcome, we would not conclude that the association between the racial characteristics of foster parents and children was paramount, although there was some tendency for mixed race children placed with white, long-term foster parents to experience more breakdowns than one might expect by chance.

It was revealed in chapter 1 that research into the problem of fostering breakdown has generally discovered a direct relationship between age and placement instability, with older children experiencing more breakdowns. As shown in table 4.4, our data broadly follows this trend, although differences are not statistically significant. Instead, children of *all* ages were vulnerable to movement. Surprisingly, well over a quarter of fosterings involving children under two at the time of placement broke down, as did a third of those experienced by the two to five age-group and approaching half of placements for children between six and 11. Indeed, the full significance of the high rate of long-term foster breakdown in the County Authority becomes apparent when we realize that the average[10] age of children at the time of placement was barely five. Interestingly, the number of adolescents in our sample of long-term fosterings is small.

Particularly important is the finding that the group experiencing most instability is the six to elevens – children such as our case study, Paul. Other studies of child welfare services have also highlighted the situation of this group of 'middle-age', or 'latency', children.[11] Whereas much attention in the social work literature and on training courses

TABLE 4.4 AGES OF LONG-TERM FOSTER CHILDREN AT THE OUTSET
OF PLACEMENTS

Age	Placements that did not break down	Placements that broke down	Proportion of placements that broke down (%)
Under 2	20	8	29
2–5	46	23	33
6–11	43	37	46
Over 12	8	4	33
Total	117	72	38

concentrates on children at the extremities of the age span –
infants and adolescents – it is now becoming apparent that
those in the middle, children of primary school age, pose
quite specific problems. Children in this middle-age range
tend to stay long in care, they are particularly susceptible to
divorce of parents and emotional and educational problems
are increasingly surfacing while at primary school.

Little has been written specifically about 'middle-age'
children. What literature exists is almost entirely North
American in origin and the guidelines that are espoused
concerning child development are likely to be more
culturally-specific than the authors acknowledge. Moreover,
most studies are preoccupied with the development and
problems of boys; girls, in contrast, tend to be portrayed as
little more than an adjunct to their opposite sex.

Despite these limitations, there are two studies in particular that provide valuable insight into the developmental
needs of primary-school-age children. These assist in our
understanding why this group should demonstrate a particularly high level of breakdown in long-term fostering.
Gessell and his colleagues, for example, chart children's

development during these 'middle' years.[12] They carefully differentiate discrete stages but, generally, this period is portrayed as one of emotional transition. Children gradually become less self-centred and more aware of the expectations of others and societal norms. Problems are compounded with the onset of schooling. This latency phase develops into a period in which children become increasingly inquisitive, particularly concerning human relationships. A redefining of status relationships also occurs and the balance of influence of peers, siblings and elders is in a state of flux. Goodman, in contrast, emphasizes the latency period as essentially one in which the child's self-concept develops.[13] She maintains that this sense of self very much stems from the way in which others react to the child and, especially, meet his or her need for approval.

Clearly, from these viewpoints, we would expect children of this age-range who have been separated from their families to experience particular problems. Whereas children entering care are likely to have existing emotional problems, the turmoil associated with the latency phase will also impose additional stress. In addition, children will become more aware of their status; especially the role ambiguity inherent in being fostered. Interactions with peers may also pose problems for children who are insecure and lacking confidence. Thus, as individual identity and peer relationships develop, the child's feeling of adversity will be reinforced.

It is interesting to observe from table 4.4 that the bulk of long-term foster placements are made during these primary school years. (Although one contributory factor towards the lower incidence of breakdown in the London Borough than in the County Authority was that its children tended to be very young.) It is also significant that, if one looks at the age of children when placement breakdown actually occurs, it is *not* – as might be expected – adolescence, characterized by turbulence, defiance and other crises: a quarter of placements end when children are over the age of 12. Instead, 45 per cent of breakdowns occurred to children while in their middle years. These findings imply that we may need to reconsider some of our assumptions about childhood behaviour and further research into the needs and problems of 'middle-age' children could prove fruitful.

Categorizing the principal reasons for children's admission to care is notoriously difficult but, nonetheless, important to attempt. Our sample of children experiencing long-term foster placements had experienced a variety of precipitating factors. The most important *primary* reasons for admission, however, were neglect and/or abuse of the child – 34 per cent; mental illness of parents – 17 per cent; abandoned or deserted by parents – 16 per cent; and cases in which parents were unable or unwilling to care for the child – 13 per cent. (Since these are primary reasons for entry to care, these categories are mutually exclusive, although most children will experience a combination of these factors.) There was no discernible relationship between primary reasons for admission to care and the prognosis for long-term placements. The one exception was the relatively small number of children – 12 out of the 189 – who came into care as a result of the behaviour problems they posed: seven of these 12 fosterings broke down prematurely.

Once children were admitted to care, however, a relationship was evident between their legal status at the time they were fostered and subsequent placement outcome. Children who remained in care on a voluntary basis subsequently experienced significantly fewer (21 per cent) breakdowns than those committed by courts (44 per cent). This finding is not age-related and, in fact, legal status at the outset of placement is one of the strongest indicators of outcome that we were able to discover. Indeed, the greater use of voluntary care in the London Borough than in the County Authority contributed towards its lower breakdown rate in long-term fostering. We shall return to this theme later but these findings suggest that placements that are brought about by involving natural parents in care plans have a better prognosis than those in which a spirit of co-operation does not exist. Indeed, as we saw from our case study in the previous chapter, although Paul's mother eventually acceded to the care plan designed for her son, she was not to any great extent involved in its formulation.

It was demonstrated in the opening chapter that the earlier predictive studies of fostering breakdown, particularly the research of Trasler[14] and Parker[15], found important links between the early rearing histories of children and subsequent placement stability. In general, our evidence did not support these findings. Overall, our study population were first admitted to local authority care remarkably young – half before the age of two, and a further third between two and five – yet there was no noticeable association between age first admitted and placement outcome. Similarly, neither was there any connection between the likelihood of a long-term fostering breakdown and the proportion of a child's first three years of infancy spent living in foster care, in residential settings or in care overall.

Thus our findings indicate that, in terms of the impact on future placement stability, the adverse effects of early separation are not necessarily irreversible and children are not somehow predisposed to placement failure. In this respect, we are in agreement with others who have questioned aspects of the Bowlby thesis. But if we focus not only on formative years but, instead, on children's *overall care careers*, a rather different picture emerges. For example, there is a strongly significant relationship between the total length of time a child has spent in care and the likelihood of a long-term fostering breakdown: as many as 64 per cent of placements ended prematurely for children who, like Paul, had spent, in all, more than five years in local authority care – almost double the figure for the remainder (34 per cent). (Although it is likely to be, by definition, older children who have spent longer in care, we should remember the earlier finding that the relationship between age at time of placement and subsequent outcome is by no means unchallengable.)

Similar results apply when we consider the duration of the *current*, rather than all, care episodes. Children who had been continuously in care for long periods were more likely to experience a breakdown in long-term fostering than those whose separation was more recent. It is interesting to note, however, that time spent in care expressed as a proportion of a child's age is not significantly related to outcome. A possible interpretation of these findings is that since it is the absolute, rather than relative, period of time in care that appears significant, it would seem that the longer a Social Services Department has responsibility for a child, the more vulnerable is that individual to an unsettled experience. Moreover, these findings would suggest that to integrate successfully children such as Paul, who have been long in care, into traditional style foster homes is a hazardous process.

These conclusions are confirmed when we examine the previous placement histories of children in our study group. Unlike marriages and driving tests, where statistics indicate that second attempts are rather more successful than first, our evidence clearly reveals that children who had previously experienced (presumably unsuccessful) long-term foster placements – a quarter of cases in our sample – were more likely to witness breakdown in a subsequent placement than those for whom it was an initial fostering: comparative figures were 56 per cent and 32 per cent. Thus, the greater incidence of failure implies that initial, unsuccessful fosterings tend not to act as a learning experience to equip children to cope with the stresses of living in another family. Instead, it would seem that the added damage inflicted by a failed placement can compound children's existing problems and, hence, make future stability more unlikely.

If we examine further children's care histories, the situation becomes particularly interesting when we consider the impact of a residential experience. Despite the widespread unpopularity of residential care and its alleged damaging effects on children, our evidence clearly indicates that children who were living in a residential setting prior to placement in a long-term foster home experienced significantly fewer breakdowns (34 per cent) than those of their peers who transferred directly from home or from another foster household (51 per cent). Thus, an interlude in the more territorially netural environment of a children's home before living with another family seems beneficial. This may assist children to prepare emotionally for the drastic upheavals occurring in their lives. Another possibility is that introductions into foster homes are more effectively undertaken from a residential base, when social workers are assisted by residential staff. There are, however, important differences in outcome depending on the functions of the previous residential experience and the length of time that a child has lived there. Indeed, as shown in table 4.5, a relatively brief stay – less than a year – was particularly effective. Children such as Paul who linger in residential care, on the other hand, are noticeably less successful and it can be particularly difficult to readjust to family life after several years in a group care setting.

TABLE 4.5 LENGTH OF TIME PREVIOUSLY SPENT IN A RESIDENTIAL SETTING

Time previously in residence	*Placements that did not break down*	*Placements that broke down*	*Proportion of placements that broke down (%)*
None	17	22	56
Up to 1 year	44	14	24
More than 1 year	55	36	40
Total	116	72	38

The length of time that children in our sample had been awaiting a foster placement ranged considerably: four per cent of long-term placements were organized with remarkable haste and the child moved in within a week of fostering first being mooted; a further 14 per cent materialized within a month; half took between one and six months; while one child in every six who was eventually fostered had been awaiting an appropriate family for more than a year. No clear relationship was evident between time awaiting placement and subsequent outcome, although it is interesting to observe that of the 16 children whom it had taken more than two years to foster, a high proportion – nine (one of whom was Paul) – were unsuccessfully placed.

Similarly, once what were thought to be suitable foster parents were found for our sample of children, there is no indication of an optimum period of introduction. Before moving in, the average period of acquaintance between foster child and foster family was a month; a period we felt to be unexpectedly brief. Although there is no overall trend that links the degree of preparation with future outcome, several findings are of interest. For example, in eight per cent of placements, child and foster parents were already well acquainted. (It should be remembered that the group of children under discussion excludes those fostered with relatives.) Children knew these foster parents because they had lived with them previously, they had fostered a sibling or were family friends. Significantly, only one of these placements subsequently broke down. A second observation is that a surprising number of placements were made remarkably hastily – a fifth of children had packed their toys and toothbrushes and set off within a week, and another nine per cent did so within a fortnight. Unsurprisingly, these placements were particularly unsettled, with breakdown rates of 50 per cent. Thirdly, a somewhat disconcerting finding is that in a fifth of placements for which reliable information was available, social workers never personally met the foster parents prior to the day of arrival. Instead, the selection was based entirely on information provided by colleagues or placement officers.

We have now considered a number of variables concerning the characteristics, early rearing histories and care experiences of our study population of children and examined their link with the outcome of planned long-term foster placements. Overall, our search for predictive, biographical factors was largely unrewarding and the variables that we investigated were not found to predispose children for fostering breakdown at some future date. We discovered no unequivocal relationship between placement outcome and sex of children; their racial origins; age; reason for admission to care; age first admitted to care; and early care history. In this respect, our investigation parallels much other social science research that has found it increasingly difficult to explain *social* behaviour – such as delinquency or absconding from residential institutions – entirely in terms of *individual* characteristics.[16] Matters of definition, administrative and organizational factors have also been found to be relevant. Indeed, our investigation highlighted the importance of children's care experiences; particularly the preparation for the foster placement. We shall, therefore, extend the sociological focus of this study and consider further the *social processes* by which children's care careers are managed. Thus, we turn to the second of the perspectives underlying our analysis, the significance of children's social networks.

Children's social networks

Of the numerous dimensions concerning children's social networks that could be selected, we decided on the following four: children's links with natural families; the liaison role of social workers; relationships with siblings; and continuity in schooling.

Recent research both in Britain and North America has demonstrated the importance for children in care of maintaining family contacts.[17] With the exception of a small number of children, whose parents pose an immediate risk, children who are in regular contact with their families have been shown to be more settled in their placements; to be able to accommodate more easily relationships with other adults; and to be more likely to return home, having spent shorter periods of time in care. Initially, we approached the question of family contact by exploring the proximity of long-term foster placements to children's natural parents. It was discovered that the average distance was eight miles. To some, this may appear reasonably local – being no more than a Saturday morning jaunt to the nearest out-of-town hypermarket. However, it was confirmed in our interviews that for many parents the inaccessibility of placements, let alone other problems, posed a genuine barrier in keeping in touch with their children. As one natural mother explained:

I found it ever so hard to get out to where they put him. The buses were about one every hour and I had to go up with all my shopping and that. The social worker said at the start she would take me up there if I wanted but I never heard any more about that and I didn't like to put on her. I don't know if it's right but I always felt like they were testing me out and seeing if I would keep going up there even though it wasn't easy. I wasn't going to let them beat me.

It is difficult in many authorities to find local foster families but this unapproachability also reflects the 'anti-family' ideology that is the historical legacy of social work and still pervades the service.[18] This view is implied in the above quotation and, indeed, underlies the case study presented in the previous chapter. There was in our data no clear evidence, however, of a relationship between distance of placements from parents and the likelihood of breakdown: matters are, obviously, more complex. Nevertheless, there was one exception to this generally inconclusive result: one child in every nine was placed a very long distance from his or her original family – more than 100 miles – and 48 per cent of these fosterings subsequently broke down, compared to 35 per cent of all others.

As other studies have consistently revealed, the frequency of contact between children in our sample and natural parents was depressingly low.[19] Details are presented in table 4.6. Unlike Paul, only five per cent of children enjoyed at least fortnightly contact with their parents while, in contrast, as many as 40 per cent (to the knowledge of social workers) had *no* contact whatsoever for the duration of their foster placement. Restrictions on contact imposed by social workers were only partially accountable for this inactivity: in a fifth of all cases, the frequency of meetings was controlled. There was, however, no discernible correlation between the imposition of restrictions and the eventual outcome of fosterings.

TABLE 4.6 LEVELS OF CONTACT BETWEEN CHILDREN IN LONG-TERM FOSTER PLACEMENTS AND NATURAL PARENTS

Level of contact	Placements that did not break down	Placements that broke down	Proportion of placements that broke down (%)
Weekly	0	1	100
Fortnightly	8	1	11
Monthly	1	3	75
Three-monthly	32	17	35
Six-monthly or less	26	15	37
No contact	50	34	40
Total	117	71	38

Excluding categories with small numbers that are, therefore, unreliable, there is from table 4.6 some indication of an inverse relationship between the degree of parent contact and levels of breakdown. However, the differences are insufficient to be statistically significant. Although numbers (24) are relatively small, more interesting perhaps is the finding that cases in which meetings between parents and children *increase* over time – from whatever original level – are noticeably *less* likely to break down than those in which links remain constant or diminish.

Clearly, the role of social workers is central in facilitating relationships between parties involved in the fostering process and we now turn to the extent of their intervention. Our 'intensive' material provides us with greater scope to examine the nature of social workers' efforts; but, at this stage, we shall search for any connection between the extent of involvement and placement outcome. First, we focus on social workers' visits to the foster households. Our firm conclusion from scrutinizing casenotes was that social workers responded to the situations presented by long-term foster placements rather than acting as initiators: a finding that has been confirmed by other recent child care research, which has emphasized the 'reactive' nature of much social work activity.[20] Hence, after an initial flurry of involvement prior to settling in, if matters appeared to be progressing smoothly, most social workers would keep a low profile and visit infrequently. This was demonstrated by Judy Chamber's involvement with the Gilbeys, Paul's foster parents. Moreover, where there were staffing shortages in social work teams – and this was not uncommon in the London Borough due to delays in appointments or 'frozen' posts – it was often what were felt to be the unproblematic, long-term fostering cases that would remain unallocated to caseworkers.

These general observations are confirmed by our statistical data. On average, long-term foster households were visited by social workers every seven weeks, although the commonest interval for visits was every two or three months. To believe that foster parents can realistically obtain intensive support in half a dozen or so visits a year seems to us rather optimistic. Placements which broke down were visited much more frequently than those which endured. Some cynics might suggest that it was the increased visiting in itself that hastened the demise. Our view of social work, however, is rather more benign and the increased activity was clearly a response to the problems affecting the foster placement.

Social workers paid rather less attention to children's natural parents than they did to the foster households. Excluding cases in which parents were no longer alive, no fewer than 38 per cent of social workers and parents did not even meet. A particularly interesting finding is that there was a much reduced incidence of breakdown where social workers and parents were in contact – however frequently – than when no such relationship occurred. Indeed, this is one of the strongest factors associated with outcome and, significantly, was a noticeable feature of care management in the London Borough. As with the earlier finding concerning the apparent advantages of voluntary care arrangements, it would again seem that involving parents in care plans pays dividends for future placement stability.

A related issue concerning social work involvement is the organization of statutory reviews. Section 21 of the Boarding-Out Regulations stipulates that foster placements must be reviewed, initially, within three months and every six months thereafter. The 1969 Children and Young Persons Act extended this responsibility to apply to all children in local authority care, regardless of placement. A recent study of statutory reviews by Sinclair, undertaken in a local authority in the Midlands, revealed some rather disconcerting findings, particularly concerning children who were fostered. Although reviews were quite regularly undertaken, half of all reviews pertaining to foster children were perfunctory exercises, lasting less than ten minutes; no children or their families participated in any reviews; and in barely 11 per cent of reviews were children even informed that such a meeting was taking place.[21]

We did not systematically investigate the content of reviews but our impressions are that Sinclair's findings have wider relevance than the one Department which she studied. We did, however, analyse the frequency of statutory reviews held for children in our sample of long-term foster homes and seek to relate this to placement outcome. For placements lasting more than six months, we calculated the number of reviews held as a proportion of the total number that *should* have been convened if they had been arranged six-monthly. Findings revealed that the full complement of statutory reviews was held in only 15 per cent of cases;

three-quarters of reviews were arranged for 15 per cent of children; half were held for 30 per cent of children; while the figures for a quarter and fewer than a quarter of reviews were 26 per cent and 13 per cent respectively. It was clear that statutory requirements were frequently disregarded and, following Sinclair's research, these findings should arouse concern.

The frequency with which reviews were held parallels the findings for social workers' visiting: placements that were in difficulty, particularly those eventually destined for failure, were more frequently scrutinized. Indeed, the full complement of reviews was held for 40 per cent of long-term fosterings that eventually broke down, compared with only six per cent for those that were sustained. This supports the earlier finding that serious problems in placements tend to be evident early on and implies, incidentally, that it is only when fostering is in jeopardy that this statutory requirement is likely to be fulfilled. It is also significant to point out that in 15 (nine per cent) of the 167 placements that lasted over six months, no reviews were held whatsoever and, not unsurprisingly, this lack of ongoing assessment was rewarded with a 73 per cent failure rate for those cases.

We now return more directly to the question of children's social networks and examine relations with siblings. The significance of siblings is little explored in the social work literature.[22] We know that approximately half of all children entering care (three-fifths of the under elevens) are accompanied by one or more brothers or sisters. Furthermore, recent research into children's homes revealed that these establishments serve important functions in catering for sibling groups and reuniting families that have split up.[23] It is clear that there are often difficulties in accommodating sibling groups within the same foster home; social workers are forced to make some difficult decisions in balancing the needs of individual children for family placements with the desire to keep sibling groups intact. We also saw the impact on Paul, our case study, of being re-united with his older brother.

We felt it important, therefore, to examine the situation of siblings in some detail. One hundred and forty-five children in our sample of long-term fosterings had siblings in care and their placement arrangements are detailed in table 4.7.

TABLE 4.7 PLACEMENT ARRANGEMENTS FOR CHILDREN WITH SIBLINGS

Arrangement for siblings	Placements that did not break down	Placements that broke down	Proportion of placements that broke down (%)
Child has siblings in care but is living with *none* of them	34	34	50
Child has siblings in care, *some* of whom are living in the same foster placement	32	12	26
Child has siblings in care, *all* of whom are living in the same foster home	22	11	33
Total	88	57	39

The results reveal that there is a much higher failure rate – 50 per cent – when children are completely separated from siblings than when they are accompanied by brothers or sisters. It would seem, therefore, that the presence of others of a similar status may help to relieve some of the associated stresses. The influence of peers has been identified in other areas of social research, particularly in mental health and studies in deviance and the sociology of education, and it is interesting to observe similar features in operation within the child care system.[24] However, the social work literature (written, of course, by adults) is preoccupied with the importance of children's relationships with adults: social workers, foster parents, residential workers, assorted therapists, and so on. Our findings suggest that a less condescending approach – particularly to older children – would be justified and that the significance of peer support is greater than has previously been thought.

These conclusions are reinforced by the existing literature, mostly in the field of psychology, on siblings. These studies emphasize the importance of birth order, gender and 'age-spacing' when considering sibling relationships. Generally, however, relations between brothers and sisters are portrayed as inclusive and containing high levels of intimacy. Sutton-Smith and Rosenberg, for example, describe sibling relationships as a shield against the adult world and claim that they communicate more effectively with each other than with their parents.[25] Furthermore, Dunn has shown the way in which sibling relationships can be simultaneously disruptive yet supportive. For children in care, who have often experienced inadequate parenting, sibling relationships may provide an important compensatory experience. As we have seen from table 4.7, however, something like half of our long-term fostering study group with siblings in care were totally isolated from them. In this context, children in long-term foster homes were further disadvantaged and the higher incidence of placement breakdown where siblings are separated is understandable, especially where it is the care process that has led to the decision. One thirteen-year-old girl that we interviewed said the following about sibling relationships:

Me and me two brothers, they're both younger than me, got put into care five years ago when me mum died. Me dad didn't give a damn, he never has. To start with we got put in a children's home but after a while they said we were going to be fostered and it meant me going to one family and the two of them going somewhere else. I cried for days and I haven't seen them for two years. Me social worker said they've got to be given the chance to have a fresh start. I've got nobody now. We used to fight and that but we'd been through a lot together and we understood each other. I'll find them when I'm eighteen, nobody will be able to stop me then.

Of course, peer relationships are formed not only with siblings but also in other contexts and especially important as an arena for developing roles and social networks is the school. The educational problems of children in care and the educational implications of social work decisions are areas that have received little research attention. Thus, it is encouraging to note that the Economic and Social Research Council, DES and DHSS are promoting research into these and related issues.[26] Our study was unable to examine in detail the educational experiences of children in our sample; we did, however, interview several teachers for the 'intensive' stage of the research and investigate continuity in schooling for the larger sample. Results for school-age children in our long-term fostering sample are revealed in table 4.8.

TABLE 4.8 CHILDREN EXPERIENCING CHANGES IN SCHOOL WHEN MOVING INTO THE FOSTER PLACEMENT

Weather changed school	Placements that did not break down	Placements that broke down	Proportion of placements that broke down (%)
Changed school	45	40	47
Did not change school	20	6	23
Total	65	46	41

Some research findings require little elaboration; for example, the discovery in a study of approved schools which, when investigating after-care arrangements, revealed that over 40 per cent of children could not even name their social worker.[27] Our findings on the discontinuity in education experienced by our sample of children are equally disturbing.

When moving to their long-term foster home, no fewer than three-quarters of children also changed school. Furthermore, other evidence from our study reveals that of children experiencing placement breakdowns, four-fifths joined new schools when departing from the foster home. Apart from the profound disruptions to learning that must have resulted, the disadvantages of discontinuity in schooling are apparent from table 4.8: the breakdown rate for fosterings in which children also changed school was double the level for those where continuity in education was present.

We saw in our case study the social and emotional, let alone educational, problems experienced by Paul when joining his new school. He was breaking into a new social setting and into established friendship hierarchies. As we argued on the influence of siblings, the significance of the peer group for children cannot be overemphasized. It is a purveyor of cultural norms, providing a sense of security and the opportunity to explore an assortment of roles. Bruner has written, 'Friendships are often the source of children's greatest pleasures and deepest frustrations'[28], while it has been deduced from a number of psychological studies that peer relations can compensate for unsatisfactory parenting.[29] However, research has also stressed the importance of stability in peer relations over time. The effect on a general population of children of moving home has been described as one of loneliness, depression, instability and anger and they will often mourn the loss of close friends.[30] Consequently, deep friendships may be avoided to avoid the fear of loss. Clearly, this will pose particular problems for many children in care as they move between placements, neighbourhoods and schools.

The findings in this section have demonstrated the important relationship between the maintenance of children's social networks and placement continuity. We noted the degree of disruption to which children in our sample moving to long-term foster homes were subjected. Not only did they see little of their parents, move to different neighbourhoods and join unfamiliar households, the majority were also isolated from siblings and forced to join new schools, tackling complex negotiations of status and stigma. Such radical upheaval would be expected to cause chaos in the lives of the most 'integrated' – to use Winnicott's term[31] – of people, yet those in our society who are probably least equipped to cope are subjected to this social merry-go-round. Some changes in the family lives of children in care may be inevitable but our evidence clearly indicates the importance, wherever possible, of keeping constant at least some, aspects of children's social networks.

Peer support – for example, from siblings or school friends – would seem to be valuable in helping children cope with adversity; it is also likely to be of benefit in the longer term if such relationships are maintained. It is clear, therefore, that change and uncertainty are more easily managed if they are restricted to specific areas rather than if one's entire social life disintegrates – the reality, regrettably, for many children in care and a situation that is often exacerbated by the care process.

Placement-related factors

Our focus of attention now moves away from *children* in our sample to the third of our underlying themes, placement-related factors, and we consider the households children were to join. This stage of the investigation, however, was hampered by the paucity of information kept on foster families. Despite careful searching, we found no files for many foster parents (almost a quarter) and those that were found – in contrast to the voluminouss outpourings on children – would usually consist of a letter of application and a few sheafs of A4. The location of foster families' records also provides a useful insight into their status within Social Services Departments: they would usually be retained alongside files on *clients*. Hence, particularly in the County Authority, foster parents were very much perceived as clients – recipients of social work services – rather than colleagues and this may partially account for a number of problems highlighted in this research.

An interesting development in recent years has been for foster parents to be more broadly representative of all socio-economic groups rather than disproportionately to derive from working class communities.[32] No statistically significant link was found between placement outcome and social class of long-term foster parents, however, and breakdowns are more evenly distributed. More revealing was the link between the age of the foster mother at the time of placement and the likelihood of breakdown. No evidence was found to relate age of foster father to outcome, yet foster mothers over the age of forty witnessed noticeably fewer unsuccessful placements than their younger counterparts: 17 per cent compared with 37 per cent. A number of interpretations could be proposed for this finding; the obvious one being that older foster mothers may be more experienced in child care matters. Alternatively, another explanation could be that, with older foster mothers, children are less likely to experience conflicts about the role ambiguity of foster parents and the respective positions of natural and substitute parents. Our investigation discovered on numerous occasions that difficulties ensued when foster parents were perceived by children as attempting to replace natural parents. Paul, for example, despite being repeatedly cajoled, adamantly refused to call his foster parents 'mum' and 'dad' and this caused him much anxiety. When age differences are more pronounced, this problem may be minimized.

We also felt it important to explore the experience and preparation of foster parents prior to the current placement and both variables were found to yield interesting results. Overall, we discovered in both agencies a high level of wastage of foster parents: residential care has been criticized for the rapid movement of child-care workers yet, perhaps surprisingly, our evidence suggests that wastage rates for foster parents are not dissimilar. More than three-fifths of our long-term foster parents, including Mr and Mrs Gilbey, had been fostering less than a year and for the overwhelming majority of these, the current placement was their first. In contrast, only 18 per cent had been fostering for more than five years.

One of the most pronounced findings in our study was that long-term foster parents with less than a year's experience suffered disproportionately many more breakdowns – 42 per cent – than those who had been fostering longer, whose comparative rate was barely a quarter of this figure (10 per cent). These results clearly indicate the value of retaining and nurturing foster parents. It is also significant to note that very few foster parents – only four – had previously experienced a placement breakdown. This, presumably, implies that when disruptions occur, a high proportion of couples also decide to sever their relationship with the Social Services Department. A more sympathetic and constructive approach to the problem of breakdown might help retain scarce fostering resources.

Induction training for long-term foster parents had been introduced only relatively recently in our study authorities; hence numbers who had experienced this form of preparation were few and our results are inconclusive. Nevertheless, such an investment seemed to have advantages in terms of placement stability. Breakdown rates for those who had attended regular preparatory meetings were lower than would otherwise have been expected.

It will be recalled from chapter 1 that other studies of foster home breakdown have uncovered the relevance of the foster parents' own children, particularly where these are very young or similar in age to the foster child. Despite the many developments that have undoubtedly occurred since the formation of Social Services Departments in the early 1970s, our evidence revealed that this situation remains unchanged. One child in six was placed with foster parents who had a child, or children, of their own under the age of five and 55 per cent of such placements broke down, in comparison with only half this rate – 27 per cent – when no such child was present. Parker has identified some of the factors affecting the supply of foster parents, including the greater preponderance of lone-parent families and the more widespread participation of women in the labour market.[33] Future recruitment of foster parents may, therefore, increasingly emanate from families in which women, whether through choice or necessity, remain at home to provide for young children; ironically, as we have seen, a group that reveals high levels of placement breakdown.

In reading social workers' records, we were impressed by the frequency with which reference was made to research findings concerning the undesirability of placing children with families in which there was already a child of the foster parents within five years of age of the foster child. However, when placements were actually made, such a consideration was frequently disregarded. Indeed, despite the rhetoric of assessment and emphasis on individual 'needs', children clearly received what was available and no fewer than 48 per cent of our sample, including Paul Thornton, were placed in a household in which there was a natural child within five years of age. As Trasler and Parker predicted 20 years ago (see chapter 1), over 40 per cent of such placements ended prematurely, compared to only 25 per cent of those where no such child was present.

However, if we consider the presence of other foster children in the placement apart from the foster child's siblings, a rather different pattern emerges. Many observers assume fostering to be an intimate, individual experience between foster child and foster parents; in contrast to the chaotic camaraderie of residential care. Yet, in only one placement in six was no other child – natural or fostered – present; while in as many as a third of households, unrelated foster children were *in situ* at the outset. The largest number of other foster children present at various times during a placement was 20, most of whom were accommodated on a short-term basis. Incidentally, this fostering did not break down. Indeed, although one might have assumed the opposite, long-term placements in which unrelated foster children are present are more successful in terms of endurance than those in which adult care is undivided. (This finding applies independently of other variables but especially where foster parents have children of their own.) Indeed, excluding foster children's siblings, households in which no other foster children were present revealed a 40 per cent breakdown rate, in comparison with only 20 per cent of those where others were present. Even more surprisingly, perhaps, households in which other foster children were present who were within five years of age of members of our sample, were significantly less likely to experience breakdown than arrangements where no such child was present: comparative figures were 38 per cent and 9 per cent.

Conclusion

In conclusion, these findings concerning the significance of placement-related factors indicate that it may be necessary to re-examine a number of assumptions commonly held about long-term foster care. In particular, it would seem that it is not the individual nature of the experience that is significant but that advantages accrue from other foster children being present. This would reinforce our earlier findings concerning the importance of peer support; and foster children – as with siblings – may be able to assist each other in a common experience. If we accept that the presence of other foster children is advantageous, it may also be wise to reconsider some of our thinking concerning residential care. The group setting may not be a disadvantage; relationships with adults may not be as all-important as one might think. Instead, peers are a valuable source of short- and long-term support, particularly in a context in which children have repeatedly been failed by adults.

Our findings also portray an essentially 'supply-led' view of long-term foster care. In contrast to seeking to link placement outcome to characteristics of *children*, where we discovered few significant indicators, we saw that the way in which a child's care career was managed could have an impact on future placement stability. In addition, a variety of placement-related factors proved relevant. Fewer long-term fostering breakdowns were found to occur with foster mothers over the age of 40; foster parents who had previous experience; and those who had attended preparatory training. Our results also confirmed the findings of earlier studies, outlined in chapter 1, highlighting the dangers inherent in placements in which competition is present in the form of foster parents' own children who are very young, or of a similar age to the foster child. Having demonstrated, following an interval of some 20 years, that these factors still apply, we would urge those responsible for organizing long-term foster placements not to ignore them.

Finally, it is necessary briefly to return to the contrasting levels of success in long-term fostering between the County Authority and the London Borough where, it will be recalled, the breakdown rate in the former was double that for the latter. As we saw earlier, our analysis revealed that the more specialist approach towards fostering adopted in the London Borough did not, in itself, account for this success. Instead, other variables that we have considered throughout this chapter explain differences in outcome. Nevertheless it was noticeable that, in three major areas, the approach towards fostering in the London Borough differed from that in the County Authority and it is on these factors that much of the variation in success depends.

Initially, there was a clear difference between the ages of children, with more planned long-term placements in the London Borough involving the under-fives. Older children were more likely to be placed in specialist types of fostering than in the County Authority. Secondly, the London Borough made greater use of voluntary care procedures than did its county counterpart. And, finally, this more 'inclusive' approach towards fostering was also reflected in greater contact between children and natural parents and between the latter and social workers. Thus, it is to these three features – *age, legal status* and *parental involvement* – that much of the difference in long-term fostering outcomes between the London Borough and the County Authority can be attributed.

Notes

1 See note 12 to chapter 2.
2 See p. 4.
3 At the time of writing, research into children 'home on trial' is being undertaken by Professor Roy Parker, School of Applied Social Studies, University of Bristol.
4 See for example Department of Health and Social Security, *Children in Care of Local Authorities*, Year ending 31 March 1983, England, DHSS, 1985.
5 See S. Millham, R. Bullock, H. Hosie and M. Haak, *Lost in Care: The Problems of Maintaining Links Between Children in Care and their Families*, Gower, 1986.
6 See D. Berridge, *Children's Homes*, Basil Blackwell, 1985.
7 Table 4.2 and, where appropriate, all other subsequent tables have been checked for statistical significance by using the 'chi-square' test. This is a statistical measurement which indicates the probability of results occurring purely by chance.
8 J. Rowe, H. Cain, M. Hundleby and A. Keane, *Long-Term Foster Care*, Batsford, 1984.
9 One useful publication is C. Petrie, *The Nowhere Girls*, Gower, 1986.
10 Unless otherwise stated, the statistical measurement of 'average' used throughout this study will be the median.
11 For example A. Gesell, F. Ilg and L. Bates Ames, *The Child from Five to Ten*, Harper Row, 1977; M. Goodman, *The Culture of Childhood*, Teachers' College Press, 1974; M. Pollack, *Nine Years Old*, MTP Press, 1979; J. Williams and M. Smith; *Middle Childhood, Behaviour and Development*, Macmillan, 1974; M. Shepherd, B. Opperheim and S. Mitchell, *Childhood Behaviour and Mental Health*, University of London Press, 1971.
12 Gessell et al., *The Child From Five to Ten*.
13 Goodman, *The Culture of Childhood*.
14 G. Trasler, *In Place of Parents*, Routledge and Kegan Paul, 1960.

15 R. Parker, *Decision in Child Care*, Allen and Unwin, 1966.
16 For example: M. Rutter and H. Giller, *Juvenile Delinquency*, Penguin, 1983; S. Millham, R. Bullock, K. Hosie and R. Frankenberg, 'Absconding', *Community Home Schools Gazette*, nos. 7 and 8, vol. 71, 1977, pp. 280–91 and 325–37.
17 Millham et al., *Lost in Care*; D. Fanshel and E. Shinn, *Children in Foster Care*, Columbia University Press, 1978.
18 See Berridge, *Children's Homes*, chapter 2.
19 See for example Department of Health and Social Security *Social Work Decisions in Child Care: Recent Research Findings and their Implications*, HMSO, 1985.
20 Ibid.
21 R. Sinclair, *Decision Making in Statutory Reviews on Children in Care*, Gower, 1984.
22 Exceptions are B. Sutton Smith and B. Rosenberg, *The Sibling*, Holt, Rinehart and Winston, 1970; K. Konig, *Brothers and Sisters*, Rudolph Steiner Publications, 1958; J. Dunn, R. Plomin and D. Daniels, 'Consistency and change in mothers' behaviour to young siblings', *Child Development*, vol. 56, no. 2, 1986, pp. 348–356; J. Dunn and C. Kendrick, *Siblings: Love, Envy and Understanding*, Harvard University Press, 1982; H. Nix, 'Sibling relationships in older child adoptions', *Adoption and Fostering*, vol. 7, no. 2, 1983, pp. 22–8.
23 Berridge, *Children's Homes*.
24 See for example: W. Hartup, 'Peer interaction and social organisation' in P. Mussen ed. *Carmichael's Manual of Child Psychology, vol. II*, J. Wiley and Son, 1970; J. Bruner, M. Cole and B. Lloyd, *Children's Friendships: The Developing Child*, Fontana, 1980.
25 Sutton Smith and Rosenberg, *The Sibling*.
26 See S. Jackson, *The Education of Children in Care*, Report for the Social Science Research Council, University of Bristol, 1983. Further work is being undertaken on the education of children in care by Jane Aldgate at the University of Oxford.
27 S. Millham, R. Bullock, P. Cherrett, *After Grace – Teeth*, Human Context Books, 1975.
28 Bruner et al., *Children's Friendships*.
29 See for example W. Hartup, 'Peer interaction and social organisation'.

30 H. Swick Perry and M. Ladd Gewel eds, *Harry Stack Sullivan: The Interpersonal Theory of Psychiatry*, Tavistock, 1955.
31 C. Winnicott, *Child Care and Social Work*, Codicote Press, 1964; *Deprivation and Delinquency*, Tavistock Publications, 1984.
32 See Rowe, *Long-Term Foster Care*.
33 R. Parker, 'Foster care in context', *Adoption and Fostering*, no. 3, 1978, pp. 27–32.

5

Short-Term and Intermediate Foster Care: Shirley – a Case Study

In the following two chapters, we consider types of foster care other than the traditional long-term variety: namely short-term fosterings and intermediate placements, including 'specialist' schemes. First, however, it may be helpful to present a second case study – Shirley Stone – which illustrates a number of the factors that are associated with unsuccessful placements. It is difficult to describe Shirley's fostering as belonging to a particular category because, as we shall see, the expectations of social worker and foster parents differed.

Shirley is a nine-year-old with blonde hair and blue eyes but her good looks and innocent appearance belie a more troubled interior. Shirley's home life, as well as that of her younger brother Kevin, has been far from comfortable. Her mother knew neither of her own parents and spent her complete childhood in Barnardo's homes. She looks back at her own upbringing with a surprising degree of nostalgia but recognizes that her hard and impersonal upbringing has imposed limitations on her own parenting abilities. As a result of an industrial injury, Mr Stone has been unable to work for many years and the financial difficulties that have resulted have aggravated the family's problems. In addition, Mrs Stone has a history of mental illness, which has required periods of hospitalization. Consequently, the level of family stress has been high and numerous health, education and welfare representatives have expressed concern over the children's development.

When younger, Shirley and Kevin were received into voluntary care for brief periods on three occasions when family problems became particularly acute. She has usually been cared for in children's homes, although she did spend three weeks with foster parents at the age of four and a half. The most recent and prolonged admission to care occurred three years ago when Shirley was six. Mrs Stone had been in a profoundly depressive state for some time and, two weeks previously, had made what was her second suicide attempt. Shirley was being particularly difficult at the time. She was causing conflicts between her parents by being extremely affectionate towards her father while deliberately ignoring her mother. Her enuresis had progressively worsened and she had started to soil during the day. She was also destructive of her clothing and household belongings, and acting unpleasantly towards her brother.

Matters came to a head one Sunday evening while Mr Stone was away at the local pub. Shirley was refusing to go to bed and her mother was in a distressed state. Since both children were subject to a Supervision Order at the time and the family's social worker – Mr Clarke – had stressed that, if she ever wanted help, Mrs Stone should contact him, she took his advice and phoned the Social Services Department. Unfortunately, family crises do not always coincide with office hours and the telephone call was answered by the duty social worker who, while offering sympathy and reassurance, regretted that Mrs Stone could not be put through to her social worker; neither would it be possible for anyone to come out to visit her until the following morning.

Mrs Stone insists that she does not remember exactly what happened next but police reports state that, after receiving several phone calls from neighbours, complaining that she was dragging her screaming daughter late at night along the middle of the road, a car was sent out to apprehend Mrs Stone and Shirley. On arrival, the two police constables found Mrs Stone to be highly distressed and disoriented and to be carrying a large kitchen knife in her pocket. Her explanation at the time was that, as no one would come out to see her, she was taking Shirley to the city centre to see the duty social worker. Furthermore, as there had been several reported 'muggings' in her neighbourhood recently, she thought it inadvisable to be out late at night without adequate protection.

The police were understandably concerned, not only for the mother's welfare but particularly for Shirley. They returned mother and daughter home in order to assess the situation more fully, where they were met on the doorstep by a rather surprised and rapidly sobering Mr Stone, who had returned to find Kevin left alone. He managed to calm his wife and put Shirley to bed and the police, satisfied that the immediate crisis was resolved, and that the child was not in imminent danger, decided no further action was needed other than to inform the family's social worker, Mr Clarke, the following morning.

Social workers tend to approach Monday mornings with an even greater sense of trepidation than do the rest of the workforce, as they often arrive refreshed at their desks, to find them littered with memoranda describing how carefully arranged plans for clients have disintegrated over the weekend. Mr Clarke found himself in a similarly unenviable position this fateful spring day and, on phoning the police and being informed of the details of what had happened the previous evening, became extremely anxious about Shirley and Kevin's situation. The Department, at the time, had recently tightened its child care procedures, owing to a spate of recent publicity in the national press, and these events may have had some bearing on the decision of Mr Clarke and his team leader to remove Shirley and Kevin from their parents' care in order to safeguard their protection.

Shirley is removed from her parents

As it would seem that the immediate crisis was resolved and Shirley and her brother were not in imminent danger, there was some debate within the team as to whether a Place of Safety Order was the appropriate legislation to invoke in this case. Nevertheless, to the consternation of teachers and fellow pupils, Shirley and her brother were removed from their junior school the following morning by the social worker and were driven off to a local children's home. On calling at the school that lunchtime to collect his children, Mr Stone was met by Shirley's embarrassed classteacher, who found herself in the invidious position of having to explain to him what had happened an hour earlier. She also handed over copies of the Place of Safety Orders, which had been left by the social worker for Mr Stone, setting out the legal basis under which action had been taken. Shirley's teacher was asked by Mr Stone to read and explain to him the contents of the Orders; he was clearly agitated and repeatedly insisted that 'the welfare' had kidnapped his children.

The next few hours saw a flurry of activity as the Stones hastened to the Social Services Department, barged into the team room, demanded a confrontation with Mr Clarke and insisted on seeing their children. Mr Clarke responded that, because of Mrs Stone's unpredictable behaviour, Shirley and Kevin had been brought into care and, in order to let them settle into their placement, the parents would not be allowed to see their children until the following weekend – some five days away. The Stones were initially stunned at hearing this and stormed out of the building, voicing a few well-chosen epithets. In a highly distressed condition, Mrs Stone, supported by her husband, visited the local Citizens' Advice Bureau and was recommended to make contact with a solicitor, which they immediately did. It is significant that the parents of children who come into care are themselves often socially isolated, unpopular with neighbours and bereft of family support. This applied very much to Shirley's parents but Mrs Stone did know, from her many years of involvement with Social Services, several mothers whose children were in care. She therefore spent the whole of the following day visiting these contacts to ask them if they had come across Shirley and Kevin in any of their visits to foster or residential homes in the city.

This rapid consumer survey, however, did not lead to the information that Mrs Stone was seeking so, first thing on Wednesday morning, she returned to the Social Services Department to seek out Mr Clarke. The social worker informed his flustered client that he would take her and her husband to see Shirley and Kevin on Saturday afternoon. Mrs Stone remonstrated strongly but soon became more subdued when informed in no uncertain terms that, if she wanted her children to be returned to her, co-operation with the social work plan was a prerequisite.

As arranged, Mr Clarke collected Mr and Mrs Stone – and some of the children's clothes – the following Saturday and took them to the children's home in the centre of the city where they had been placed. The family had a tearful reunion but Mrs Stone was reassured to discover that the residential home was a Barnardo's establishment – it will be remembered that she herself had been a 'Barnardo's girl'. After sitting uneasily with Shirley and Kevin for about twenty minutes in a television lounge, in full view of staff and other residents, Mr and Mrs Stone anxiously began looking at their wristwatches, each other and then at their social worker and suggested that they should leave. Prior to their departure, they were ushered into an office, where they were introduced by Mr Clarke to Miss Cooper, the officer-in-change of the children's home.

After being given a brief introduction to the establishment, the first question asked by Mrs Stone was how often would she and her husband be permitted to visit Shirley and Kevin. To their surprise, Miss Cooper explained that, within obvious limits, they operated an 'open door' policy and that parents could visit their children whenever they wished. She also added, to Mr Clarke's embarrassment, that she was surprised that they had not visited already that week as, in her experience, parents are important in helping distressed children to settle into unfamiliar surroundings.

Both children seemed to adapt reasonably well to the children's home; they continued at their original school and saw their parents regularly. However, Mr Clarke found Mr and Mrs Stone generally unco-operative and, in consultation with his team leader, doubted whether it was in the children's best interests to return home immediately. For this reason and despite Mr and Mrs Stone's vehement opposition, the Social Services Department successfully applied to the local juvenile court for Interim Care Orders, which were followed by full Care Orders on the grounds of neglect.

Two months later, a case conference was called in order to consider Shirley and Kevin's long-term future. This was chaired by the Divisional Director of Social Services and attended by Mr Clarke and his team leader, Miss Cooper (the head of the children's home) and Shirley's class teacher. Mr and Mrs Stone were not invited to attend; indeed, they were unaware that a meeting had been called. Interviews with participants in the meeting revealed that there was disagreement about how best to proceed. Mr Clarke and his social work colleague doubted the long-term viability of the Stones' home and were concerned that Shirley and her brother would either 'drift' in care or experience repeated short-term admissions. Thus, they proposed that the children be placed in a medium-term foster home for six months to a year and the family situation be carefully scrutinized. It was also, paradoxically, agreed to control natural parents' access in order to ensure the stability of the placement. The officer-in-charge of the children's home is recorded in the conference minutes as being opposed to this plan; by this time she had struck up quite a relationship with Mrs Stone and anticipated that her fondness for her children, her persistence and, not least, her antipathy towards the Department would cause major problems for any foster parent.

Despite these objections, Mr Clarke's view won the day and he began a search for foster parents which, as with our earlier case study, proved to be not quite so easy as he had anticipated. In preparation for this move, Mr Clarke told Mr and Mrs Stone that their access to Shirley and Kevin at the children's home was to be restricted; at first to two visits a week and, subsequently, to only one visit over the weekend. Mrs Stone was furious when informed of these decisions and could not understand why her children could not remain at the Barnardo's children's home and see their parents regularly. In a fit of rage, she told Mr Clarke never to set foot in her house again and stormed off to see her solicitor, saying that she would challenge the Care Order at every opportunity – which she subsequently did.

Shirley's file in the social work office contains copies of correspondence that ensued over the next few weeks between Mrs Stone, the Director of Social Services and an impressive range of other figures and agencies, including her local MP, DHSS headquarters in London, the Prime Minister and, perhaps the most politically astute move, Esther Rantzen. Instead of being interpreted as reflecting her concern about her children, Mrs Stone was perceived as a trouble-maker. She revealed in interview that she was informed on a number of occasions that, if she did not continually meddle and would only co-operate with the social worker, she would stand a much better chance of Shirley and Kevin being returned. This placed Mrs Stone in something of a dilemma. As she explained:

It's alright him saying that but I'm their mother and it goes against my natural instincts just to stay away. Anyway, I trust that social worker about as far as I could throw him and in the past I've co-operated with them and it's got me nowhere. I've learned that you only get what you want if you stand your ground and fight them.

Nevertheless, despite these ominous signals, Mr Clarke went ahead with his search for foster parents for the children and his painstaking investigations eventually produced only three possible couples. None of these were completely satisfactory; indeed, they were each willing to accept only one child rather than both and Mr Clarke reluctantly accepted that Shirley and Kevin would have to be accommodated separately. Kevin was soon placed with one of the three couples, where he has remained to the time of writing. For Shirley, on the other hand, because of her demanding nature, Mr Clarke was ideally seeking a placement in which she would be the only child or, if not, one in which she would certainly be the youngest.

Shirley's foster placement

Eventually, it was agreed that Shirley be placed with Mr and Mrs Murray: experienced foster parents who had taken children from the Department for seven years, although they had not attended training sessions and did not wish to become involved in the fortnightly foster parent support group meetings. At the time the placement was under consideration, the Murrays were not fostering and only had their sons, aged fourteen, ten and seven. They had for some time been indicating to the Social Services Department that they would like a young girl placed with them to balance their family and this was becoming difficult to resist. Significantly, the Murrays' willingness to work with the natural parents of foster children does not seem to have been a major factor in selecting the placement; although, as we have seen, Mr Clarke was hardly spoilt for choice.

Plans therefore went ahead for Shirley to be placed with the Murrays. The introduction to them took place over a period of six weeks – Shirley had by then been living at the children's home for four months – and initial contact went well. There are two points in particular concerning the way in which Shirley's placement with Mr and Mrs Murray was initiated that have an important bearing on the development and eventual outcome of the placement. First, there was some uncertainty about what the social work plan for Shirley actually was. From the social worker's perspective – revealed in interview, in case notes and the conference minutes – the foster placement, as revealed earlier, was envisaged to last between six months and a year, by which time Mr and Mrs Stones' situation would, it was felt, be clearer. Mrs Stone, on the other hand, insists she was told – as with Kevin – that the foster placement was to be for a maximum of six months before Shirley could be returned to her; over this period, she was to receive intensive social work and psychiatric support in order to help her offer a more stable home base. Mr and Mrs Murray, when interviewed, expressed yet another view: they were led to believe by Mr Clarke, they claimed, that Shirley's placement with them was to be short-term and that she would, therefore, stay no longer than two months.

The second pertinent factor concerning the way in which Shirley's placement was organized concerns the foster parents' own social worker. For two years, the Social Services Department had been operating a system whereby foster parents, in addition to being visited by children's social workers, were also independently allocated a social worker from the team responsible for the locality in which they resided. Mr and Mrs Murray's own social worker was a Mr Jenkins who, when interviewed, freely admitted that he was uncertain what his exact role with the foster parents was supposed to be. He had recently joined the Department and had quite enough to do without attempting to fulfill what appeared to him to be an unspecified and marginal role. Nevertheless, despite being uncertain about his exact responsibilities, Mr Jenkins expressed strong views about the way in which Shirley's placement with the Murrays was made. He was completely unaware that the placement was being considered and only found out a month later when a form from County Hall crossed his desk. Mr Jenkins' own words more than adequately summarize his feelings at the time: 'I was appalled when I found out – there's no other word for it. I was bloody angry at Dave Clarke and told him so on the phone, but he only backtracked and made excuses.

I couldn't believe it when I saw that form and I looked such a fool on top of everything else.'

Apart from Mr Jenkins's indignation, there were more serious reasons why, in this case, Departmental procedure should not have been bypassed. Another social worker, who some months previously had placed a short-term foster child with Mr and Mrs Murray, had written and sent to Mr Jenkins a strongly worded report, questioning whether the Department should continue to use the couple as a future fostering resource. More specifically, this report had stated that the foster father in particular was too authoritarian and inflexible to be a foster parent; the couple wanted to foster primarily in order to satisfy their own family needs; and they were unwelcoming towards the natural parents of children. Shirley's social worker, when making the placement, was unaware of this critical report and Mr Jenkins stated emphatically that, if he had been able to express his view, he would probably have advised against it.

At first, Shirley seemed to settle well with the Murrays and their three sons, revelling in the surfeit of material benefits and male attention. Soon, however, a different side of the youngster started to emerge. Shirley began to react jealously against the boys and stole or destroyed books and other items of their property. She also repeatedly mentioned how much she missed her parents and Kevin, whom she saw infrequently. Her enuresis and soiling became more severe at this stage and occurred both during the day and at night. Mrs Murray comments on her behaviour at the time:

I've never seen anything like it. We've had difficult kids but never anything like Shirley. She started ripping the wallpaper, she'd shout and swear at the neighbours – my husband works on a building site and he said he heard things from her that his mates would never use. I remember her wetting herself was also a terrible problem at the time and we had her pants drying all over the place. One day I was right at the end of my tether and I told her, joking like, that if she wet herself again I'd make her wear her knickers over her head. That afternoon, I saw her coming down the street after school and I couldn't believe it – she had her pants on her head. All the neighbours could see. I asked her what she thought she was doing and she said she'd wet herself at school and thought she'd save me the trouble!

Life did occasionally have its lighter moments and Mr and Mrs Murray were clearly very fond of Shirley, yet they realize that this period was extremely difficult and desperately unhappy for them. They also claim that Shirley was distressed by her parents' visits and that her behaviour deteriorated markedly after she had seen them. Interestingly, when interviewed, Shirley's class teacher gave a different view and said the child was better behaved at school after she had seen her mother. Mrs Murray claimed that 'Shirley would be a little angel if it wasn't for that mother'. On the foster parents' insistence, Mr and Mrs Stone's access to their daughter was curtailed to once every three weeks and they were not allowed to go into the Murray's house but, instead, had to meet Shirley on the doorstep. On return from their Saturday afternoons out, Mrs Murray recalls standing outside the house for up to half an hour talking with Mrs Stone, while Mr Stone sat in their car listening to the sports results on the radio. When it was time for them both to depart, Mrs Stone would shout 'Goodbye' to her daughter who, by then, was totally involved in her favourite television programme 'Jim'll Fix It' and, despite having eaten a Wimpy and chips barely an hour previously, had made considerable inroads into a pile of sandwiches. Although she was critical of her in many respects, Mrs Murray did recall that whenever Mrs Stone brought presents for Shirley, she would also include something for the three sons.

Schooling

Shirley's problems persisted unrelentingly and it is significant that these were also reflected in her behaviour at school. When she joined Mr and Mrs Murray, because of the distance she would otherwise have to travel, Shirley also changed schools and, as a later interview with her new class teacher – Mrs Burgess – revealed, she found this transition extremely difficult. Shirley was shy in groups and, because of her tantrums, became unpopular; furthermore, word somehow got around school that she was 'in care', which attracted teasing from certain of her peers. Mrs Burgess graphically described the problems she faced with Shirley when she first arrived. The school was provided with no background information on Shirley; Mrs Burgess was, therefore, unaware which schools she had previously attended and the educational and behaviour problems she had posed. It was some weeks later that Mrs Burgess was called to her headmistress's office to be presented with the largest file on a child – consisting of child guidance and educational psychologists' reports – that she had ever seen.

Many mornings, Mrs Burgess reported that she had no choice but to have an actual phsical confrontation with Shirley who, at this stage, was still in her early years of primary education. On the days in question, Mrs Burgess, in a most vivid account, explained what would happen:

Shirley would enter the classroom, she would be white and her hands and teeth would be clenched as tight as they could. I could see that she was full of anger that was bursting to get out. Eventually, I learned the best way to tackle her: I would go up to her and hold on to her tight and reassure Shirley that everything was alright and she could get angry with me if she wanted to. I would then hold on to her for dear life while she screamed and cried and hit me on the chest – once she'd done that, which took about five minutes, everything was perfectly alright and we'd have a good day together. The other remarkable thing was all the other kids in the class understood – and they were only about seven years old then, remember. I explained to them what was going to happen and they sat there quietly and never caused a bit of trouble until it finished – then the little sods started!

Problems persisted for Mr and Mrs Murray, although solutions were rather more elusive. Little support and guidance was forthcoming. Mr Clarke would visit once every three weeks and his weekly phone calls implied to Mr and

Mrs Murray that he was only watching over the placement rather than wishing to become actively involed in it. Consequently, when problems mounted, the foster parents approached members of their family for guidance, rather than contacting the Social Services Department. At one stage, in desperation, the couple approached Mrs Burgess at Shirley's school and sought her help: she went over possible techniques, including ignoring attention-seeking behaviour, anticipating and preventing problems and introducing a system of 'behaviour modification', involving keeping a chart on the wall and offering rewards in the form of different coloured stars. To her dismay, Mr and Mrs Murray returned to Mrs Burgess two days later, saying that they had tried all of her suggestions but to no effect.

By now, two important developments began to take place. First, Shirley had been with Mr and Mrs Stone for six months and, having understood from the outset that the placement was to be short-term, the foster parents began to demand rather more forcibly how long Shirley was to remain with them. The second important development was that, having been restricted in their access to Shirley and remaining unconvinced that their daughter's return to them was imminent, Mr and Mrs Stone decided formally to challenge the Care Order. This appeal was unsuccessful but did have one important outcome: the court recommended that Mr and Mrs Stones' access to their daughter should be increased to once a week rather than once every three weeks.

The fostering breaks down

When interviewed, Mr and Mrs Murray stated that during the week following the court case, Shirley's behaviour deteriorated dramatically – she continued tearing wallpaper, her soiling worsened, she was lying and stealing and antagonism between her and the three sons increased. She also repeatedly insisted that she wished to return to her parents and be reunited with her brother Kevin. Mrs Murray found the stress increasingly difficult to bear. Her husband was working long hours and the bulk of child care responsibilities fell on her. Consequently, her health suffered: she was experiencing blackouts and her asthma worsened. On visiting her family doctor, Mrs Murray was informed that she was suffering from nervous tension because of Shirley and that, if the child remained with the family, the effects would become more serious.

Mr and Mrs Murray reluctantly reached the decision that Shirley would have to go; although, if they did this, they were concerned that the Department would look upon them as having failed and might not place foster children with them in the future. For this reason, Mr and Mrs Murray were reluctant to notify Mr Clarke of the severity of problems they were experiencing. He only learned of the crisis that was looming, therefore, when he answered the telephone one morning and was told by a highly distressed Mrs Murray that she had done everything she could for Shirley. She added that they could forsee no end to these problems, as Shirley had not been moved on from what was supposed to have been a temporary placement, and that she and her husband would be grateful if Shirley could be removed from them immediately.

Mr Clarke was completely taken aback by this piece of news and immediately drove round to see Mrs Murray – Shirley being at school. The foster mother was very reluctant to lose Shirley but insisted she had suffered enough. Mr Clarke proposed that the family be given a break from Shirley for a couple of weeks as the strain must be difficult to bear. Mrs Murray replied that this would have helped earlier in the placement – indeed, she was previously unaware that such options existed – but matters had now deteriorated to such a degree that there was no alternative than for Shirley to leave. Mrs Murray did agree, however, to keep Shirley until the end of the week in order to allow time for alternative arrangements.

Over the next couple of days, the options for Shirley were carefully considered by Mr Clarke and his team leader:

another foster placement at this stage was ruled out as it was felt that Shirley would take some time to recover from the shock associated with the move. Significantly, return home was also seriously considered, yet Mr Clarke felt there was insufficient improvement in home circumstances. The third possibility was a residential placement. It was eventually decided that the final option – residential care – was the most appropriate and plans were made to place Shirley in the local 'Children's Centre'; a home with observation and assessment that had recently changed its name. On arrival at the residential home, according to its senior social worker, Shirley was very distressed and cried constantly for the first two days. However, one advantage of the residential placement was that it was close to her school and Mrs Burgess and Shirley's classmates were able to provide an important source of continuity and support, as well as ensuring that disruption to her education – where she was beginning to make some progress – was kept to a minimum.

Conclusion

Shirley's unfortunate experience highlights a number of issues that, as we shall see, indicate problems in fostering. Initially, the placement hardly had the best of beginnings; the different parties – foster parents, natural parents and social worker – had contrasting expectations about the purpose of the fostering and its intended duration. Hence, as we saw, the placement lasted much longer than the foster parents had envisaged and considerable problems ensued. Bureaucratic confusion was also evident surrounding the exact role of the foster parents' own social worker and the way in which this prevented important information concerning the placement from being divulged.

Clearly, the restrictions on access between Shirley and her parents were a particular source of conflict. It is evident that these occurred in an attempt to safeguard the continuity of the placement and to placate the foster parents, rather than to act primarily in the long-term interests of Shirley and her family. We also saw that, although it was not the social worker's intention, Shirley was separated from her brother Kevin, while the enforced change in school introduced additional complexities.

It is also significant that Shirley was the only child fostered with Mr and Mrs Murray and that conflicts arose between her and the three Murray children. Jealously and constant bickering were reported. Finally, the role of residential care is again apparent in coping with fostering failures.

Having examined in detail the situation of one particular foster child, let us now consider the extent to which the problems we have identified apply more generally to a broader range of fosterings.

6

Short-Term Fostering

In our consideration of types of foster care other than the traditional, long-term variety, we begin by focusing on planned short-term fostering; defined in the Boarding-Out Regulations, it will be recalled, as family placements designed to last up to eight weeks.[1] Short-term fostering is the most common initial placement selected for children entering care. It is preferred for younger children and groups of siblings, particularly those admitted to care because of situational problems but who, nevertheless, are soon expected to return home. In a recent study of the child care system, for example, one child in every three entering care was first placed in a short-term foster home and some 70 per cent of these were discharged home in a matter of weeks once family problems were resolved.[2]

Our analysis of short-term fostering proceeds rather warily as this whole area remains remarkably uncharted. Despite careful searching and with the exception of a useful but brief exercise by Jassal, we have been unable to reveal any previous major study of this area.[3] It is significant that, whereas the troublesome minority of children in our child welfare system attracts disproportionate research input – for example, delinquents and those retained in secure accommodation – services for the overwhelming majority who pose few serious control problems, such as short-term fostering and children's homes, have received scant attention.

Breakdown rates

Overall, our survey of social workers' records focused on 156 planned short-term fosterings. Classifying the outcome of these placements is particularly complex. In contrast to long-term foster care, where we saw that, especially in the County Authority, premature ending of placements was not uncommon, a relatively small number of short-term fosterings broke down within the eight week period – only 16 (10 per cent) of the 156. A more serious problem, perhaps, was that intended short-term placements often lasted much *longer* than envisaged; indeed, this might be considered in a different sense of the term a 'breakdown' in the social work plan. For example, 28 per cent of children were still present in the same household after six months, and half of these survived a year. The foster parents who accommodated a 'short-term' foster child for 15 years before he moved to a flat of his own, must have been impervious to the problem of fostering breakdown, let alone the procrastination of his five social workers. But as we saw in the previous chapter with our case study, Shirley Stone, difficulties can arise when placements are unexpectedly prolonged. Of the 58 fosterings that lasted significantly longer than anticipated, that is over three months, 14 (24 per cent) eventually resulted in a crisis with the foster parents insisting on the child's removal. (None of these returned immediately to the family of origin.) Clearly, there are benefits from minimizing the number of moves a child experiences while in care, particularly if early return home is felt to be imminent. Yet we shall see in our interviews with foster parents, as with Mr and Mrs Murray, the considerable problems that can arise when objectives and expections of a placement are unclear.

Thus, in total, 19 per cent of planned short-term placements 'broke down' in so far as children were removed in a manner that was inconsistent with the social work plan. Either social workers were strongly dissatisfied with the progress of a placement or foster parents insisted on a child's removal. It is also important to stress that there is little evidence of a breakdown in short-term fostering hastening the process of rehabilitation; if this were the case, without wishing to be unkind, one might welcome the profound disarray of social workers' plans. Instead, only one child (three per cent) immediately returned to her family of origin following the placement breakdown. A quarter of the total went to other foster homes, while the remainder – over 70 per cent of all cases – including Shirley, were transferred to residential establishments, mostly children's homes. Again, the importance of residential care and its interrelation with fostering is evident. Where such disruption occurred to social work plans, the relatively straightforward nature of most short-term care admissions became more problematic and the possibility of a longer absence from home increased.

In contrast to our findings concerning planned long-term fostering, comparative breakdown rates for short-term fostering between the County Authority and the London Borough were similar – 20 per cent and 17 per cent respectively. As before, however, there was *no* evidence of a decrease in unsuccessful placements in recent years and the breakdown rate in short-term fostering appeared constant over time. Notwithstanding the advances that have taken place in other areas of child-care work, the degree of placement stability offered to children has, again, remained unchanged and this finding may be received with disappointments.

Circumstances in which breakdowns occur

We saw in chapter 4 that social workers perceived the majority of long-term placements to be proceeding satisfactorily. As shown in table 6.1, evidence on short-term fostering produces similar results.

TABLE 6.1 SOCIAL WORKERS' PERCEPTIONS OF SHORT-TERM FOSTER PLACEMENTS

Rating	Placements that did not break down[a] (%)	Placements that broke down[b] (%)	All placements (%)
Highly satisfactory	30	9	26
Generally satisfactory	52	32	48
Both satisfactory and unsatisfactory	16	45	21
Generally unsatisfactory	1	9	2
Highly unsatisfactory	1	5	2

[a] Number of cases, 99.
[b] Number of cases, 22.

Excluding the 35 placements for which casenotes provided insufficient information, the figures in table 6.1 reveal that social workers were satisfied with three-quarters of short-term fosterings. Feelings were mixed about a fifth of fosterings, whereas social workers were seriously concerned about the quality of only four per cent of placements. It is also clear from the table that social workers' assessments are closely linked with the outcome of placements. However, although it might appear that social workers were intimately acquainted with the development of short-term fosterings, other evidence reveals that their knowledge was far from detailed. Indeed, excluding those placements for which no perceptions were recorded, it is clear that many breakdowns, such as Shirley's, were unanticipated. For example, in a third of placement terminations, records contained a strong indication that the fostering was in jeopardy; in a further quarter, some forewarning was noted; whereas in more than two-fifths of placements, social workers were completely unprepared for the breakdown and satisfactory progress had previously been recorded.

Hence, as with our long-stay findings, the study of short-term fosterings discovered that social workers seriously misjudged a small but, nevertheless, significant proportion of placements. Further damage is thus inflicted on children who, presumably, entered care for a stable and rewarding experience. For example, apart from reinforcing emotional problems, we shall see that half of the over fives also changed schools on leaving the short-term foster home. Thus, a number of children in foster homes of varying qualities are living in circumstances about which their social workers are largely unaware. We may need radically to reappraise the way in which such placements are assessed and maintained.

Reasons for breakdown

As in chapter 4, we also attempted to categorize from social workers' casenotes reasons for short-term fosterings running

TABLE 6.2 REASONS GIVEN IN SOCIAL WORKERS' RECORDS FOR SHORT-TERM FOSTERING BREAKDOWNS

Type of reason	(%)[a]
Child-focused	30
Natural parent-focused	0
Placement-focused	37
Child + parent-focused	0
Child + placement-focused	23
Parent + placement-focused	0
Child, parent + placement-focused	3
Other	7

[a] Number of cases examined, 30.

into difficulty. This complex area will be considered in greater detail in chapter 8, but our exploration of records yielded some interesting findings that could be further explored in interviews. Results are shown in table 6.2.

It is immediately noticeable that the pattern of findings for short-term breakdowns presented in table 6.2 is not dissimilar to that for long-term fostering shown earlier. Our investigation of casenotes revealed that children, even those who were very young, could pose considerable problems for short-term foster parents and temper tantrums, extreme swings in mood, attention-seeking behaviour and other signs of emotional disturbance were not uncommon. Shirley is a good example. Indeed, as our analysis reveals, the primary reasons for the breakdown of 30 per cent of placements were essentially 'child-focused'.

As before, it is also interesting to observe that the natural parents and wider families of children had little responsibility for the demise of placements. Shirley's mother, for example, was vehemently opposed to the social work plan for her daughter, yet did not seek to jeopardize the foster placement. However, as with our long-term population, we can once again see from table 6.2 the relevance of what can be described 'placement-focused' reasons for breakdowns. These, it will be recalled, are factors that emanate primarily from the foster placement and much of the responsibility for failure in such circumstances must lie with the social work agency that selected the placement. 'Placement-focused' reasons accounted for the termination of 37 per cent of short-term fosterings and, in association with problems caused by the child, for a further quarter of breakdowns.

Our case-study, presented in the previous chapter, does not provide the clearest example of 'placement-related' factors contributing towards breakdown. Yet, we should not overlook the way in which, due to local government bureacracy or malpractice or both these factors, an important report questioning the suitability of the foster parents was not seen by the placing social worker.

As in chapter 4, it may again be helpful to provide some illustration of placement-related reasons for breakdowns and, of the 11 cases within this category, the following are brief descriptions of four examples that were selected at random:

Girl (aged 8) Foster parents experienced marital problems and decided on a trial separation. It was felt inappropriate for the girl to remain either with the foster mother or her husband.

Boy (5) Foster parents, following a three-year wait, were approved as prospective adopters. This foster child, who had been living with the couple for eight months, had to move in order to accommodate the baby and was transferred to a children's home.

Girl (aged 18 days) Baby was placed in short-term foster placement for five weeks. Foster parents had already arranged a holiday and the baby had to be transferred to another foster family.

Boy (6) and Girl (3) These siblings were removed by their social worker after a stay of a month, following a letter written by a neighbour of the foster parents, who alleged that the children were being ill-treated.

Clearly, the majority of breakdowns in short-term placements – including those in which we have identified 'placement-related' reasons for termination – cannot be attributed solely to the foster household. Some observers might also question the use of the term 'breakdown' for fosterings which, from the outset, were intended to be only temporary. Nevertheless, it was apparent that unplanned changes in short-stay placements were extremely disruptive to social work planning and hampered children's relationships with their families. A consequence of a fostering breakdown was often that children became absorbed more deeply into the care system and subsequent placements were more closely protected in an attempt to avoid repetition. As one social worker in the London Borough wrote following a short-term placement that had broken down:

John had to be removed from the Gibsons today. It's the last thing I wanted and it puts me right back to square one, but it was too much for her to cope with the two other babies she's got. Mrs Weekes said she'll have him next week and I'm going to ensure that things are more stable from now on. We're aiming to get John back to his mum in a month or two but I feel I'm going to need to protect Mrs Weekes from her for a while. The worst thing now would be Mrs Weekes having to cope with Julie's unpredictable nature as well. I think it's best for John if he sees a bit less of his mum to begin with and we can reassess how it goes from there.

Parents were frequently bemused by what they saw as unnecessary movement; the welfare of their child seemed beyond their control and, following placement breakdown, social workers often adopted a more defensive attitude towards parents' involvement. However, in mitigation, it should be stated that short-term fosterings were often selected at very short notice and social workers were powerless to influence where vacancies arose. Furthermore, placements were often required in the midst of a crisis, and the timing let alone nature of the resolution of the problem was often unclear. A degree of risk is, thus, unavoidable. Yet, it would seem reasonable to assume that the more widespread use of contingency planning prior to reception into care might have helped avoid some of the problems that resulted.

Characteristics, early rearing histories and care experiences of children

As with the investigation of long-term fostering, our search for biographical factors that would predict subsequent placement outcome was largely unrewarding. As before, boys outnumbered girls by three to two but breakdown rates between sexes were comparable. Similarly, although there was a slight tendency for black children to experience more fostering failures than their white or mixed race peers, results were not statistically significant. We shall see later that information on short-term foster parents was particularly sparse; hence, a number of our findings have to be tentative. Nevertheless, from our admittedly small numbers, we could find no evidence that transracial placements involving black children were any less successful than situations in which they were living with black couples. Given the heterogeneity of black cultures and identities, which many observers fail to acknowledge, one would not have expected to discover otherwise. Black foster parents – particularly those prepared to offer short-term placements – were a scarce resource in the London Borough. Yet, although some two-thirds of black and mixed race children were placed with white, short-term foster parents it is, perhaps, significant that we discovered only one instance of a white child placed with a black family.

Short-term fostering is preferred for young children who enter care and the average age of this population of children was barely three years. There was, however, as with long-term fostering, no statistically significant relationship between age at time of placement and outcome; the one exception being the small number of fosterings – 18 – involving adolescents, seven of which proved unsuccessful. The majority, some 70 per cent, of our short-term group found themselves in voluntary care and, unlike our long-term study group, no association was discovered between legal status and placement stability. Moreover, there was no discernible relationship between outcome and reasons for admission to care. However, the precarious nature of short-term fostering for adolescents is again highlighted by the finding that five of the 13 placements for youths, who entered care because of the control problems they posed, ended abruptly.

In addition, as we discovered with our long-term population, the early rearing histories of children provided little evidence for future fostering outcome. In some two-thirds of cases, the current placement was their first experience of care. There was no relationship between age first admitted to the care system and placement stability although, as shown above, the prognosis for the 13 adolescents who, on entering care, were located in short-term foster homes, was poor. No pattern was evident between fostering outcome and the proportion of early years spent in residential settings, in other foster homes or in local authority care overall. Thus, as in chapter 4, we would conclude that early experience of the child welfare system does not, somehow, seem to predispose children for particular placement outcomes and social workers have considerable influence in shaping future care experiences. Of course, depending on one's view of the operation of our child care services, this conclusion may be welcomed or received with a degree of unease.

If a longer-term perspective is adopted, we also find that broader features of a child's care experience are not closely related to the outcome of short-term fosterings. For example, unlike long-term placements, the total time a child has spent in care is not significantly related to outcome; neither is it when expressed as a proportion of a child's age. Also, the period of introduction to the household and the degree of contact between social worker and foster parents are not statistically related to outcome. However, an interesting finding is that short-term foster care is more likely to succeed when it is used as a first placement on admission to care than when a child is transferred from elsewhere, particularly where the previous placement was residential. It will be recalled that this happened to our second case study, Shirley Stone. Indeed, the failure rate for those 27 children who were moved from a residential establishment to a short-term foster home was over 40 per cent – almost treble the rate for other children.

We investigated more closely those cases where children were moved to a short-term foster home from a residential setting, and a number of important features emerged. For example, the children had spent only short periods in residential care (mostly children's homes) – for half of them, it had been less than a week. They were admitted to care in the midst of a crisis and, in most cases, residence was not the preferred option. Thus, these children were transferred to a short-term foster home at the first opportunity to await a more permanent placement. Three further observations are relevant. First, a high proportion of children in these circumstances were subject to Place of Safety Orders: 40 per cent compared to 10 per cent of the total population of children experiencing short-term fostering. As recent research has suggested, the rather dramatic process by which this legislation is selected and enacted – as with Shirley – may not be in children and their families' best interests.[4]

A second observation on children moved to short-term fostering from a residential setting is that a high proportion – almost two-thirds – were living with siblings while in group care and, in the majority of circumstances, these were subsequently separated when moving to the foster home. Indeed, we saw that Shirley and her brother Kevin were parted in this way. Finally, it is clear from our investigation that children often found the rapid series of changes profoundly unsettling: entering care at very short notice, then a few days in a residential setting before moving to a temporary foster placement. The 11 children whose fosterings broke down – mostly emergency admissions, it should be remembered – thus lived in four different environments in a matter of weeks; a curious interpretation of 'child care' and as effective a precursor to emotional, social and educational disintegration as one could possibly concoct.

Children's social networks

As with the analysis of our long-term data, we find that a number of features concerning the maintenance of children's social networks – particulary social workers' efforts in this direction – are relevant to the outcome of short-term fosterings. We begin by considering factors affecting the relationship between child and natural parents. Initially, it is apparent that most short-term placements are reasonably local – two-thirds being within five miles of home. The likelihood of breakdown, however, was not linked to proximity; a discovery that also arose, it will be recalled, when we analysed long-term placements.

TABLE 6.3 LEVELS OF CONTACT BETWEEN CHILDREN IN SHORT-TERM FOSTER PLACEMENTS AND NATURAL PARENTS

Level of contact	Placements that did not break down	Placements that broke down	Proportion of placements that broke down (%)
Weekly	30	3	9
Fortnightly	12	2	14
Monthly	9	2	18
Three-monthly	12	7	37
Six-monthly or less	14	3	18
No contact	48	11	19
Total	125	28	18

It is interesting to observe from table 6.3 that those children in regular contact with their families, as in chapter 4, seem less likely to experience unsuccessful short-term foster placements. However, the results are not statistically significant and caution should be taken over their interpretation. But there is no such doubt concerning the impact on placement outcome of access restrictions between parents and children. Cases in which the frequency of contact was limited by the Social Services Department (17 per cent of all placements) were more than three times as susceptible to failure as placements in which no such controls were imposed. Obviously, such restrictions are not arbitrarily applied but it would seem that the management of aspects of a case can have an important bearing on its development, especially as reasons for entry to care are not associated with breakdown. We saw, for example, the difficulties caused by limiting the contact between Shirley and her mother.

Similar conclusions emerge when we consider social workers' involvement in short-term fosterings. In direct contrast to the evidence concerning long-term placements, our findings reveal that more frequent visits by social workers to foster households is associated with fewer breakdowns. For example a minority, two out of every five, foster homes were visited at least fortnightly, yet the failure rate for these was ten per cent compared with more than double this figure, almost a quarter, for the remainder. Moreover, benefits also accrue from regular contact between social workers and natural parents: a finding confirmed, it will be recalled, in our study of long-term placements. Surprisingly perhaps in a third of fosterings the two parties never met. However where, for example, fortnightly meetings occurred, placements were again less than half as likely to end prematurely than in situations where contact was less frequent (nine per cent compared with 22 per cent). Social work activity can be expected to have only marginal impact on many social problems, particularly those of structural origin yet, as other recent research has concluded, our findings highlight areas in which activity is rewarded.[5]

We saw in our analysis of long-term fostering that sibling relationships are important in influencing placement stability and these findings are repeated here. One hundred and twelve children in our short-term group had siblings in care and the majority, 63, were living apart from at least some of them. The failure rate for these placements was 30 per cent. However, of the 49 children whose sibling groups were intact, only two fosterings broke down. Furthermore, placements in which children such as Shirley were completely isolated from siblings, were noticeably more likely to break down (26 per cent) than those in which they were accompanied by brothers or sisters. Short-term fosterings, it will be recalled, were frequently used as initial placements, and a possible interpretation of these findings is that the trauma surrounding family reconstitution and admission to care is cushioned – even for very young children – where siblings are present and, more specifically, if members of the family are not separated. As we saw earlier, other studies highlighting the importance of sibling relationships, particularly where there have been deficiencies in parenting, would support this view.

Another important earlier finding concerned the link between discontinuity in schooling and the likelihood of placement breakdown. Being a much younger population, only 65 children in our sample of short-term fosterings were of school age. On moving to the foster home, 25 of these also changed school and breakdown rates for this group were higher – 28 per cent – than for children where continuity in education was present, for whom the corresponding figure was 20 per cent. Indeed, we saw in our case study how Shirley's problems were compounded by a change in school. However, although suggesting some connection between discontinuity in schooling and placement failure, our sample size is insufficient for statistical reliability and it would be unwise to place too much emphasis on our findings in this area.

Placement-related factors

We now turn to the final of our underlying themes, namely placement-related variables. It was revealed earlier that a variety of placement-related factors were accountable for a proportion of short-term fostering breakdowns, and we shall now examine associations between characteristics of foster households and placement outcome. Unfortunately, our investigation is again restricted by the paucity of information about foster parents retained by the two Social Services Departments. One could hardly describe as extensive the files kept on long-term foster parents, yet records on couples offering short-term placements were even scantier. Indeed, for half of all intended short-stay placements, we were unable to locate any written records on foster parents whatsoever and, for those that did exist, information was often incomplete.

Obviously, records are not compiled for researchers' benefit but, in view of the considerable trust and responsibility delegated to short-term foster parents, we were surprised by the lack of documentary evidence, particularly that which evaluated the progress of previous placements. A memorable example of the allocation of short-term placements was in one Area Office, in which on the wall was pinned a heavily amended, and virtually indecipherable, list of local short-term fostering resources and their current placement situation. This resembled a rather outdated shopping list and was very much used as one.

Despite these limitations in data collection, we were able to glean at least some insights into the situation of short-term foster households. As we discovered when considering long-term fostering, in terms of socio-economic status, short-term foster parents whose occupations we were able to determine represented a broad range of social groups. Interestingly, middle-class foster parents experienced fewer placement breakdowns (13 per cent) than those involved in working-class occupations (35 per cent), although we would re-emphasize that numbers are small for statistical reliability. The average age of short-term foster parents was approximately forty years and, as with their long-term counterparts, there was a tendency for younger couples to be involved in a disproportionate number of unsettled placements. In contrast to our earlier findings, however, short-term foster parents overall were a rather more experienced group. Nevertheless, for a third of couples, the placement under observation was their first. Despite the relatively small sample size, the difference in placement outcomes between experienced and inexperienced foster parents was striking: for those with less than two years' fostering experience, 10 out of 28 (36 per cent) placements broke down; compared with only two out of 23 (nine per cent) for couples whose involvement was longer. Clearly, these figures again emphasize the importance of retaining experienced foster parents.

We saw earlier in the chapter that children's stay with short-term foster parents was often very brief; even for placements that ended as planned, approximately a third of children had moved on within a fortnight. Yet despite the temporary nature of such arrangements, an interesting discovery – as with long-term fostering – is that the presence of other children in the foster household had a significant influence. For example, four-fifths of short-term foster parents – including Mr and Mrs Murray who cared for Shirley – had children of their own living with them and the breakdown rate of these households was 32 per cent. In contrast, where such children were absent, no placements failed. This situation is particularly pronounced if natural children are very young: where foster parents had children of their own under the age of five, the failure rate rose to 67 per cent, compared to 11 per cent where no pre-school children were present.

Furthermore, the prognosis for short-term fosterings in which natural children were of a similar age to the foster child was also poor. Where foster parents' children were within five years of age of the foster child, as with Shirley, the majority – 53 per cent – ended unsatisfactorily; whereas none of the 28 placements involving no such children broke down. We saw in our investigation of long-term fostering the effect of foster parents' own children on placement outcome. It is also apparent, however, that where fosterings are an even more temporary arrangement, that perceived competition in the form of foster parents' own children would appear to be a destabilizing influence.

Once again, in spite of the limitations imposed by the paucity of records, our analysis of cases suggests that the presence of other foster children (excluding siblings) can also have a noticeable effect on the progress of short-term fosterings. As with long-term placements, it is not uncommon for other, unrelated foster children to be present at the outset of a short-term fostering; indeed, a fifth of households studied contained one other foster child, and a further quarter sheltered between two and four such children. A combination of 'short' and 'long-stay' children was not unusual. Perhaps unexpectedly, placements in which no unrelated foster children were present, as in the case of

Shirley, were almost twice as vulnerable to failure (31 per cent) as those in which other children in care were resident (16 per cent). Particularly interesting is the finding that the most stable short-term placements were those in which other (unrelated) foster children were of a similar age.

As before – but on this occasion applying to a quite different category of placements – it would seem that in a context in which foster parents' own children are likely to be present, foster children find their situation difficult to endure. Yet when peer support is available, in the form of others of a similar status, it may be easier, even for those who are very young, to cope with separation from families and to negotiate satisfactory relationships with foster parents and their own children.

Conclusion

To recapitulate, our scrutiny of social workers' records pertaining to 156 placements revealed that the majority of short-term fosterings proceeded relatively straightforwardly and most children soon moved on – mostly back to their families or to alternative placements – as originally planned. A proportion of placements were perhaps *too* successful and, in a quarter of all cases studied, children remained much longer than was envisaged. In total, only one placement in every five was terminated in a manner that was inconsistent with the social work plan. No discernible differences in terms of breakdown rates were evident between our two study agencies. Thus, within the parameters set by our study, it would seem that short-term fostering is an area of child care practice that works reasonably effectively. However, when problems arose in a placement, it was clear that social workers were not always as fully aware of their significance as they might have been, and the question of how best to supervise and support fostering recurs.

In our search for factors associated with outcome, interestingly, our findings on short-term fostering often paralleled those for longer-term placements. It was again discovered that many placement failures were not directly attributable to the problems posed by children. Short-term placements were often made in the throes of an emergency and the nature of its resolution was sometimes unclear. Yet, although there may have seemed few alternatives available to social workers, a number of placements were clearly innappropriate and when breakdown occurred the prospect of child and family reunion diminished.

Our attempt to link the progress of placements with the first of our underlying themes – the characteristics, early rearing histories and care experiences of children – was mostly unproductive. There was no clear evidence to associate placement outcome with gender, ethnicity or age of children; although, overall, the relatively small number of short-term fosterings involving adolescents were not particularly successful. Neither, as before, were the early care histories of children found to be strong indicators of the outcome of subsequent short-term placements.

More fruitful, however, as with our investigation of long-term fostering, was the exploration of our second perspective: the maintenance of children's social networks. Initially, some evidence was discovered for greater levels of parental contact to be associated with successful placements, although our findings must be viewed as tentative. Yet, the link between access restrictions and placement failure was firmly established. Other features of the social work management of cases were also connected with the outcome of short-term fosterings. In particular more frequent visiting of social workers to foster homes and to natural parents was rewarded with placement stability. Another important component of children's social networks is sibling relationships and, as with our long-term study group, the separation of brothers and sisters was found, in many cases, to result in placement failure. Furthermore, there was some indication that discontinuity in schooling could lead to breakdown in fostering; although it should be remembered that, in our study group, the number of school-age children experiencing short-stay fosterings was small.

Despite the meagreness of information that was recorded on short-term foster parents, the third of our recurrent themes, an examination of placement-related factors, also yielded some relevant findings. For example, younger foster parents and those who were inexperienced were more likely to host unsuccessful placements. Problems were also apparent regarding relationships between foster children and the offspring of foster parents, especially where natural children were very young or of a similar age to the subject. Significantly, however, as we discovered with planned long-term placements and with siblings, the presence of other, unrelated foster children seemed to provide a valuable degree of peer support that enabled placements to endure.

Notes

1   Statutory Instruments, 1955, no. 1377, *Children and Young Persons Boarding-Out*, HMSO, 1982; *The Boarding-Out of Children (Amendment) Regulations 1982*, HMSO, 1983.

2   S. Millham, R. Bullock, K. Hosie and M. Haak, *Lost in Care: The Problems of Maintaining Links Between Children in Care and their Families*, Gower, 1986.

3   B. Jassal, *Short-Term Foster Care*, National Foster Care Association, 1982.

4   S. Millham, R. Bullock, K. Hosie, *Place of Safety Orders*, Dartington Social Research Unit, 1984.

5   For example Millham et al., *Lost in Care;* M. Fisher, P. Marsh, D. Phillips, E. Sainsbury, *In and Out of Care: The Experience of Children, Parents and Social Workers*, Batsford, 1986; Department of Health and Social Security, *Social Work Decisions in Child Care: Recent Research Findings and their Implications*, HMSO, 1985.

6   See note 22 to chapter 4.

7

Intermediate Fostering

The final group of fosterings to be considered in our 'extensive' study consists of a range of 'intermediate' placements, including specialist or 'professional fostering' schemes. There has been a considerable expansion in recent years in the number and diversity of such placements. In response to the perceived limitations of traditional, open-ended fostering – particularly for older children – different fostering styles have developed, in which specific objectives of placements are more clearly identified. Thus, intermediate and specialist fostering have tended to cater for children who are more difficult to place, whether because of age, disability or behaviour. Such placements are usually designed to be medium-term in duration, although the scheme managed by the Voluntary Agency that we scrutinized also made frequent use of more permanent placements. 'Contracts' are now also widely used, making explicit the expectations and obligations of the various parties – foster parents, social worker, foster child and, perhaps also, members of his or her family.[1]

Another distinctive feature of intermediate and specialist placements is that foster parents often receive a more economically realistic reward for their contribution. Part of the explanation for the run down of residential facilities over the past ten years is that foster care has been perceived as a more cost-effective option. It is significant to note, however, that for comparable groups of children, and excluding the contribution of on-site education, the comparative, overall costs of residential care and a specialist placement are not dissimilar. Clearly when mounted, managed and supported properly, fostering is not a cheap option and should not be seen as such.[2]

Initially, we intended to differentiate in our investigation between intermediate and specialist fostering placements. However, our pilot work in the County Authority – later confirmed in the London Borough – soon revealed that the boundaries between the two are blurred. Specialist staff for recruitment and support are often involved in both and, as we have seen, enhanced payments are frequently made and written contracts have become usual. Hence, we suggest that there is little logical distinction in conceptual or professional terms between what are referred to as intermediate and specialist family placements. The continued use of the term 'special' – as in 'special fostering scheme' – for a small minority of fosterings also implies that the majority are somehow 'not special' or unproblematic. Yet our evidence from earlier chapters challenges this view. In the following discussion, therefore, we combine the medium-term, more specialist fosterings within the County Authority, London Borough and Voluntary Agency and refer to them as '*intermediate placements*'.

Breakdown rates

Detailed evaluations of the outcome of intermediate place-ments are few. One of the most important early projects was the Kent Special Family Placement Project and its driving force, Nancy Hazel, has written a number of valuable accounts of the scheme and its underlying philosophy.[3] However, as with the autobiographical accounts of the pioneers of residential communities, objective assessment is perhaps best undertaken by those who are less intimately involved. Shaw and Hipgrave have provided a useful overview of the field[4] and small scale evaluations have also been undertaken by Keefe[5], Thomas[6] and Yelloly[7]. Nevertheless, broader empirical investigations are lacking and we have discovered little relevant research with which to compare our results.

As shown in table 7.1, we scrutinized social workers' records of 126 intermediate placements within the three agencies. Owing to their shorter envisaged duration, we quantified breakdown rates in terms of whether placements survived a year.

TABLE 7.1 BREAKDOWN RATES IN INTERMEDIATE FOSTERING

Agency	Placements that did not break down within 1 year	Placements that broke down within 1 year	Proportion of placements that broke down (%)
County Authority	22	12	35
London Borough	44	8	15
Voluntary Agency	34	6	15
Total	100	26	21

Table 7.1 shows a significantly higher breakdown rate for the County Authority than for the other two agencies. As with our investigation of other types of fostering, there was no indication overall of a greater level of success in more recent years. It is interesting to consider the degree to which variations in outcome are attributable to contrasting agency practices. Multivariate analysis revealed that, independently of other variables that we scrutinized, there remained significant differences in outcome between the three par-

ticipating agencies. Analysis of the characteristics of respective child populations in intermediate placements confirmed
that this is unlikely to be the sole explanatory factor. With
the exception of age and ethnicity, there were few noticeable
dissimilarities in characteristics and care experiences
between 'intermediate' foster children in the County
Authority and the London Borough. Furthermore, those
referred to the Voluntary Agency for family placement had
more complex and unsettled care histories; a number also
posed additional problems for prospective foster parents
owing to physical disability, medical conditions or mental
handicap. Consequently, one might have expected a relatively high level of placement failure in the scheme managed
by the charitable organization which, as we have seen, was
not the case.

Now that the overall placement patterns of the participating agencies are known, it is interesting to contrast the
use of different types of fostering by the two Social Services
Departments. In the County Authority, the number of
long-term, short-term and intermediate placements in our
study was 190:85:34. Alternatively, in the London Borough,
the corresponding ratio was 58:71:52. These figures illustrate
the contrasting policies of the two agencies, especially the
greater emphasis on the early resolution of problems adopted by the latter. Another important finding, as we have
seen, is that there is a consistency in breakdown rates of the
two organizations: failure rates within the County Authority
for long-, short-term and intermediate fostering were each
higher than in the London Borough, thus suggesting some
common element. We return to these issues in our
concluding chapter.

Circumstances in which breakdowns occur

As other studies have confirmed,[8] and as our investigation of
long-term fostering revealed, placements that break down
tend to do so early on: half of all intermediate fosterings that

were eventually terminated did so in the first six months, and three-quarters within nine months. Consequently, although there was usually some longer-term plan for the child, most breakdowns arose too soon for this to be implemented. Hence, removal of the child mostly occurred in a situation of crisis rather than smooth transition to a planned sequel; an alternative care strategy had to be arranged. Indeed, in 24 of the 26 cases which broke down, children were relocated in residential settings – three-quarters of them in the so-called 'ordinary' children's homes. Once again, as with long- and short-term casualties, we observe the important role of residential care in absorbing fostering failures. We have discovered no evidence in this study to indicate that fostering breakdown speeds rehabilitation – an important finding. In principle, our fostering services may, one day, function at such a level that children's homes will become redundant. On current evidence, however, this eventuality seems some way off.

In a number of respects, our findings on intermediate fostering contrast favourably with those reported in previous chapters. The differences in resource allocation and organization associated with a more specialist approach are rewarded with encouraging results, in terms not only of eventual outcome but also of social worker participation more generally. For example, compared with our long- and short-term study groups, our examination of casenotes revealed that social workers were better informed of the progress of intermediate placements and more likely to be aware of problems.

As shown in table 7.2. social workers perceived the majority of intermediate fosterings to have proceeded satisfactorily: three intermediate placements in every 10 were believed to be 'highly satisfactory'; a third were perceived as 'generally satisfactory'; and another third aroused mixed feelings. It is interesting that this pattern of results is not dissimilar to those, discussed earlier, relating to long-term and short-term fostering. A noticeable difference, however, is that social workers were better informed throughout of

TABLE 7.2 SOCIAL WORKERS' PERCEPTIONS OF INTERMEDIATE FOSTER PLACEMENTS

Rating	Placements that did not break down[a] (%)	Placements that broke down[b] (%)	All placements (%)
Highly satisfactory	36	0	29
Generally satisfactory	36	15	32
Both satisfactory and unsatisfactory	24	62	32
Generally unsatisfactory	0	8	2
Highly unsatisfactory	0	0	0
No information	4	15	6

[a] 100 cases.
[b] 26 cases.

the progress of unsuccessful intermediate placements and table 7.2 shows a close relationship between social workers' assessments and eventual outcome. Indeed, in 22 (85 per cent) of the 26 fosterings that broke down, casenotes revealed that social workers were well aware of impending failure – a much higher level than in the two other categories of fostering that we have studied. In these the corresponding proportion, it will be recalled, was only a third.

Thus, it is encouraging to discover that, in intermediate placements, social workers were much better informed of the situation of their charges. It is also significant that the widespread use of contracts and the greater sense of partnership developed with foster parents in these more specialist schemes, enabled social workers to negotiate a clearer and more effective role than in other types of fostering. As one 'intermediate' foster parent that we interviewed expressed it:

We've been fostering a few years now but only a couple of years on this scheme. It's better all round, I think. The extra money helps of course but we also have our own special meetings where you can talk over the problems you're having. One of the biggest differences though, is that you get treated better by the social workers, you have a completely different relationship. We're expected to go along to case conferences and we have to keep notes on the progress and all that. I feel that I can confide in the social worker without having to worry that she'll use it against me.

Reasons for breakdown

In intermediate placements, the process of selection of foster parents and the allocation of children to particular households were undertaken more systematically and conscientiously than with other types of fostering. Consequently, it is significant that intermediate placements that broke down were less likely to do so for 'placement-related' reasons but, instead, problems attributed to children were more responsible. Once again, it is important to appreciate that the natural parents of children had little direct responsibility for placements that failed: indeed, *no* intermediate fosterings broke down for this reason alone.

Characteristics, early rearing histories and care experiences of children

We begin our examination of the factors associated with breakdown in intermediate placements by concentrating on the characteristics and biographical details of children. Throughout this study, the ratio of boys to girls fostered has remained remarkably constant at 3:2 and the same applies to intermediate fostering, where 76 of the 126 were boys and 50 girls. In contrast to what might be anticipated, however, there was a tendency for girls' placements to break down more frequently than those of boys – 28 per cent compared with 16 per cent – although numbers are insufficient for

TABLE 7.3 REASONS FOR FOSTERING BREAKDOWNS: COMPARATIVE RESULTS

Type of reason	Intermediate placements (%)	Long-term placements (%)	Short-term placements (%)
Child-focused	42	20	30
Natural parent-focused	0	1	0
Placement-focused	19	30	37
Child + parent-focused	4	1	0
Child + placement-focused	19	37	23
Parent + placement-focused	0	3	0
Child, parent + placement-focused	4	3	3
Other	11	4	7

statistical significance. This finding would reinforce the plea, expressed in chapter 4, for studies to explore the situation and problems of *girls* in care – particularly adolescents. Little is known specifically about this group while in care although, on leaving, research has demonstrated that their position can be highly precarious.[9]

Black and mixed-race children constituted half of all those in intermediate foster placements in the London Borough and the Voluntary Agency. It was apparent that intermediate schemes, in comparison with more traditional fosterings approaches, were able to be more sensitive to racial issues. For example, specialist workers were sometimes employed to work specifically with black families and recruitment campaigns for foster parents were often targetted at sections of the black community, including widespread use of advertisements in the black press.

Obviously, the issues are extremely complex but these

efforts appear to have been rewarded with a degree of success. Of the 20 intermediate placements involving black children (14 of whom were located with black families), only two (ten per cent) ended prematurely. Interestingly, all but five of the 32 mixed-race children were placed in white foster households; nevertheless, the failure rate for these placements was still relatively low at 19 per cent. In contrast, the level of breakdown for white children in intermediate fosterings – all with white families – was 27 per cent. Ethnicity was not, however, a focal point of our study and, in any case, owing to the relatively small numbers involved, it would be unwise to place too much emphasis on our findings. Nevertheless, it was apparent from our investigation of a number of cases involving children from ethnic minority groups that the schemes that had accumulated expertise in working with black families were achieving successful results.

If we examine more closely the characteristics of children and young people placed in intermediate foster homes, the reasons for their nomination for a more specialist approach become apparent. They were, for example, older than children placed in traditional, long-term fosterings, with an average age of years. Almost a third of children experiencing intermediate placements were, in fact, adolescents and the breakdown rate for these youths were significantly higher – 32 per cent – than those for their younger counterparts, whose breakdown rate was half this level. In comparison with long-term fostering, failure rates for adolescents do not reveal a significant improvement; if anything, the trend is to the reverse. However, it is significant that, for what we termed in chapter 4 'middle-age children' – the six to elevens – who were found to be particularly problematic for traditional fostering, breakdown levels were much lower and only four out of 52 (eight per cent) intermediate placements ended prematurely within a year. Hence, whereas the difficulties in fostering adolescents may be more intransigent, there is evidence that a more focused approach involving younger children can be more effective.

As might be expected with an older age group, Social Services Departments held full statutory control over more children in intermediate fosterings than in other types of placements: 59 per cent were subject to full Care Orders (1969 Children and Young Persons Act); 21 per cent had experienced Parental Rights Resolutions (Section 3, Child Care Act 1980); and a further 21 per cent retained their voluntary status. Although, as with long-term fostering, there was a tendency for there to be fewer failures in voluntary care cases, differences are not statistically significant. Results are similarly inconclusive when reasons for admission to care are compared with the outcome of placements. Surprisingly, remarkably few children in intermediate placements entered care primarily because of the behaviour problems they posed – only six per cent of the total. In contrast, a high proportion – 58 of the 126 – were the responsibility of Social Services following prolonged periods of neglect and/or abuse. There was no clear link, however, between reasons for admission to care and the prognosis for placements.

Another unexpected finding is that, in terms of factors associated with early rearing and care histories that we monitored, children selected for intermediate placements were not noticeably more 'disadvantaged' than those for whom more traditional, long-term fostering was the preferred opinion. But the temptation should be avoided to imply from this that children in intermediate fosterings were not a damaged group – quite the contrary. Indeed, as a group, they had experienced slightly more placement changes than children in more traditional foster homes. Some also had specific problems, such as physical disability or rare medical conditions. A more accurate conclusion from our findings is that children such as our first case study Paul Thornton, who experienced what is sometimes misleading referred to as 'ordinary' long-term fostering, were more problematic than was often believed. Social workers frequently assumed that to provide a stable fostering experience for children such as Paul would be relatively straightforward. As our findings have revealed, however, for many children this assumption was over-optimistic.

Children selected for intermediate fosterings, as we have discovered with other categories of placement, were often first admitted to local authority care at a tender age. Virtually a third of our study population first became the responsibility of Social Services while they could barely walk and 72 per cent of children were first separated in this way from their families before they began school. There was some indication of early separation being associated with the later breakdown of intermediate fostering but findings are not conclusive.

Nevertheless, there was incontrovertible evidence linking placement failure with length of time in care – both for the current, and for all, care episodes. This finding, it will be recalled, was also discovered in relation to long-term fostering. For children for whom the current care episode had lasted more than five years, for example, almost half of intermediate placements ended prematurely within a year, in contrast to only 15 per cent involving those who had been in care a shorter period. These findings clearly reveal the difficulty in providing placement stability for children with long care histories; a group whose problems seem to be remarkably resistant to social work intervention.[10] Even where specialist resources and expertise are applied, our findings here demonstrate that there is at best only an even chance of a placement surviving a year – a sobering finding, which places in context the degree of progress that has been achieved.

Unlike planned long-term fosterings, there was no link between placement outcome and previous fostering history. Intermediate placements, therefore, were equally likely to succeed or fail regardless of whether the child had previously been fostered or if he or she had already experienced a placement breakdown. An encouraging exception to this, however, was that when placements arranged and supported by the Voluntary Agency proved unsuccessful it would undertake, where appropriate, to introduce the child to another family in due course. With the benefit of hindsight, it was hoped that second placements would prove to be more reliable than the first. Indeed, four of the 40 fosterings organized by the Voluntary Agency were second such placements and none of these failed during the period of observation.

An important prerequisite of intermediate fosterings arranged by the Voluntary Agency was that children lived for a period in a residential establishment managed by the same organization. Residential workers liaised closely with the scheme's social workers and were, therefore, intimately involved in the introduction of the child to the chosen household. Including the two local authority departments, 67 per cent of children were accommodated in residential settings prior to moving into the foster home. Unlike our evidence on long-term placements, there was, however, no clear relationship between previous residential experience and subsequent outcome.

The 'difficult to place' label of many children selected for specialist foster schemes becomes clearer when we analyse how long children had awaited placements. Many *long-term* fosterings, it will be recalled, came to fruition hastily – the average interval before appropriate households were selected and the child moved in was approximately four weeks. Overall, intermediate placements took twice as long to materialize. This longer period is partially explained by the greater degree of sensitivity demonstrated when introducing a child to the intermediate foster household. But other factors were also responsible for the delay, the most significant of which was the difficulty in finding a suitable family. Indeed, 28 per cent of children had been awaiting their placements more than a year, including half of them – that is, one child in seven – who were waiting two or more years. However, no statistically reliable evidence could be discovered to associate outcome with the period awaiting placement, although there was some indication of a greater incidence of failure involving children who had waited longest.

Once suitable intermediate foster placements were discovered for our population of children, introductions tended to occur rather more carefully, and over a longer period, than with long-term placements. In most cases, the parties were acquainted for at least a couple of months before the relationship was allowed to develop into a more permanent arrangement and the child took up residence. Two observations are of particular interest. First, in eight (seven per cent) of the placements for which relevant information is available, foster parents and child were already closely acquainted. As we discovered with long-term placements, such arrangements proved to be a particularly suitable basis for fostering and none of them broke down within the year. Second, a significant minority of intermediate placements – 32 of the 126 – were organized remarkably hastily and the child moved in within three weeks. As before, not unsurprisingly, 44 per cent of these arrangements were destined for failure.

Children's social networks

Having encountered limited success in our attempts to link *individual* variables pertaining to children with the outcome of intermediate foster placements, we now consider the relevance of children's wider social networks. Initially, as with previous chapters, we concentrate on children's links with their families and begin by analysing the distance separating intermediate placements and natural parents. In comparison with our long and short-term populations, children in intermediate foster homes were placed further from their families, the average distance being approximately 12 miles. However, as we have discovered consistently throughout this investigation, there was no direct relationship between distance from natural parents and placement outcome.

Children living in intermediate placements saw more of their parents than did our long-term population but contact for the majority remained infrequent. The extent of contact is illustrated in table 7.4.

TABLE 7.4 LEVELS OF CONTACT BETWEEN CHILDREN IN INTERMEDIATE PLACEMENTS AND NATURAL PARENTS

Level of contact	Placements that did not break down	Placements that broke down	Proportion of placements that broke down (%)
Weekly	2	0	0
Fortnightly	16	2	11
Monthly	2	0	0
Three-monthly	24	2	8
Six-monthly or less	22	0	0
No contact	34	16	32
No information	(0)	(6)	(100)
Total	100	26	21

Only 17 per cent of children saw a natural parent at least monthly, while as many as two in every five had no such contact whatsoever. Unlike other types of fostering that we have examined, however, there was no evidence of greater levels of contact being progressively rewarded with fewer placement breakdowns. Yet a clear finding is that placements in which there was *no* contact between child and parents were much more likely to prove unsuccessful (32 per cent) than those in which a better relationship existed (13 per cent). Indeed, although comprising two out of five placements for which relevant information was available, four-fifths of all breakdowns in intermediate fostering occurred in situations in which there was no contact between child and parents. Obviously, family relationships are not always responsive to social workers' efforts and the rift between natural parents and their offspring may have been long-lasting. Nonetheless, of the 50 cases in which there was no evidence of parental contact with children, a quarter of these

– 12 – arose because it had been completely prohibited by the Social Services Department. Significantly, six of these 12 placements were soon destined for failure.

Thus, as our earlier findings revealed, there is no evidence that greater involvement of natural parents places intermediate fosterings at risk; in fact, our results suggest quite the opposite. Antagonism on the part of foster parents towards natural families was much less evident in intermediate and specialist schemes than in the more traditional, sometimes 'quasi-adoption' settings. Our findings throughout this study indicate the advantages of maintaining children's social networks in this direction.

Intermediate placements stimulated greater professional activity than did more traditional, long-term arrangements and this was reflected in the extent of social workers' involvement in these households. Visits from social workers to intermediate placements occurred, on average, twice as frequently as in long-term fostering, at three-week intervals. It was shown earlier that social workers tended to be well acquainted with the progress of intermediate placements and, as with long-term fostering, households that encountered difficulties received more frequent visits from caseworkers. There was, however, no clear relationship between placement outcome and the degree of contact between social worker and natural parents. An interesting finding, nevertheless – in stark contrast to our evidence elsewhere in this study – was that there were no intermediate placements in which parents and agency representatives were not in some form of contact. Although, as we have seen, having no *direct* result regarding placement stability, the work undertaken with natural families reflects the broader social-work focus and the longer-term perspective that was a feature of intermediate placements.

Unfortunately, in cases involving the Voluntary Agency, it was not always possible to corroborate this view by consulting statutory review documents, which were often retained by the Social Services Department from which the child emanated. But our clear impression was that intermediate placements were more scrupulously monitored than other types of placements that we investigated and that this was to the benefit of those involved.

An important recurrent theme in this research has been the significance of peer relationships, especially the link between the separation and isolation of siblings and the increased likelihood of placement failure. Long-term, short-term and intermediate fostering, as we have seen, are quite different. They cater for a range of children in a variety of circumstances; expectations of placements differ; their organization, and the social work involvement they require, are dissimilar. Despite these differences, the effects of sibling separation persist. In intermediate placements, for example, of those children with siblings, the rate of breakdown was significantly lower – 13 per cent – for children who were living with one or more of their brothers and sisters, than for those who were completely separated and living with *none*, where the corresponding figure was more than double – 29 per cent. Across such a wide variety of fosterings, these findings are remarkably consistent.

A further important dimension of the maintenance of children's social networks explored in this study is continuity in schooling. It will be recalled that the scheme operated by the Voluntary Agency required all children who were to be found family placements first to live for a period in a residential setting. Consequently, apart from those children who were reasonably local, many selected for the family placement programme would already have had to change school some months previously. Thus, it cannot be assumed that the impact of a *second* transfer will necessarily be the same as an initial move. Sixty-nine per cent of school-age children experiencing intermediate fosterings also changed school when moving into the household. However, perhaps partially for the reasons mentioned above, there was no noticeable effect on placement outcome depending on the degree of continuity in schooling. In the light of evidence from elsewhere in this study, however, it is pertinent to consider the balance between the benefits of a residential experience prior to placement and the disruption to children's education and peer networks.

Placement-related factors

An impressive feature of the scheme managed by the Voluntary Agency – enhancing the quality of this research even if the direct significance for the outcome of its fosterings is less easily ascertained – was the comprehensibility of its records. Unfortunately, the authors of the casenotes of the two Social Services Departments were rather less scrupulous. For this reason, information on the third of our perspectives – placement-related factors – is in certain areas, as before, unavoidably incomplete.

We discovered elsewhere that, in terms of socio-economic status, foster parents are now broadly representative of the wider community and this applies also to those offering intermediate placements. As with our earlier findings, fostering failure was no more the prerogative of certain social groups than others. Intermediate foster parents were also similar to their long- and short-term fostering colleagues in terms of age – the average being just below forty years. Interestingly, however, and in contrast to our earlier findings, there was no link between foster parents' age and placement outcome. Younger foster parents, it would seem, were no more likely than their more senior counterparts to be perceived by children – or themselves – as *replacing* natural parents. As we have seen, a more professional approach was adopted towards intermediate placements, in which foster parents were more carefully recruited and prepared, and roles and expectations were made more explicit.

It was revealed earlier that, for the majority of long-term foster parents, the placement under scrutiny was their first; those involved in short-term fostering, on the other hand, were a more experienced group. Perhaps unexpectedly, intermediate foster parents more closely resembled the former: three-quarters had been fostering less than a year and barely ten per cent more than five years. As we discovered in earlier chapters, there was a tendency for more experienced foster parents to experience fewer placement breakdowns. For example, the failure rate for intermediate placements concerning those who had been fostering less than a year was 23 per cent, compared with 14 per cent for those with greater experience. Owing to the paucity of record-keeping, however, we were unable to establish for how long some couples had been fostering. Thus, these results are unavoidably tentative.

An encouraging picture emerges when we explore the preparatory training experienced by intermediate foster parents. In contrast with the other types of fostering examined, the overwhelming majority of participants – over four-fifths – had experienced some induction training. Once again our sample size, if larger, would have provided greater statistical reliability yet the pattern in our results is clear. As with both long- and short-term placements, intermediate foster parents who had participated in preparatory training were involved in fewer unsuccessful placements – 12 out of 84 – than those whose preparation was less adequate, for whom the corresponding proportion was 6 out of 16. A finding that has been consistently reinforced throughout this research is the benefit of even rudimentary training for foster parents. As such preparation is increasingly being provided and required by social work agencies, this bodes well for the likely future effectiveness of fostering services.

We conclude our discussion of the significance of placement-related factors in intermediate fostering, as in previous chapters, by considering the impact of the presence of other children within the household. Representatives of the scheme managed by the Voluntary Agency, in particular, demonstrated an impressive knowledge of research and the wider literature on fostering and so were able to avoid some of the pitfalls to which we have already referred. Yet because of recruitment problems, compromises sometimes were made in the composition of households that were chosen and there is, therefore, an underlying consistency in our findings.

In 64 per cent of intermediate placements, foster parents also had children of their own living at home and, once again, the failure rate in such situations – 29 per cent – was much higher than in households where no natural children were present; the comparative figure being only six per cent. It is heartening to discover, however, that placements were usually avoided in which very young children were present – a policy well supported by our evidence. In only seven per cent of intermediate fosterings for which relevant information was available were natural children present under the age of five, and two of the six placements concerned soon broke down. Rather less priority, in contrast, was attributed to avoiding households in which there were natural children of similar age to the subject. A third (35 per cent) of placements had such children present and the failure rate of these households – 32 per cent – was fourfold that for arrangements where they were absent.

Intermediate placements were generally preferred by social workers where no other unrelated foster children were present. It was often alleged, understandably, that many households would be unable to fulfil the emotional requirements of more than one seriously disadvantaged child; although, as we have seen elsewhere, our evidence would suggest that peer support can be important in helping children to live in other people's households. Nevertheless, few other foster children were present at the outset of placements (only 14 households) and it would, therefore, be inappropriate to comment on their impact.

Conclusion

An examination of the 126 intermediate placements in our wider sample of fosterings revealed some interesting differences from our long-and short-term findings. In a number of respects, these results are more encouraging than elsewhere. For example, social workers were better informed of the progress of placements and less likely to be unprepared for problems developing in intermediate foster households. More rigorous selection procedures also ensured that what we have termed 'placement-focused' reasons for breakdown were more scarce. Introductions to intermediate placements were managed more sensitively over a longer period. Children also were in more regular contact with their natural families, which was discovered to lead to greater stability in placements. Furthermore, social-work involvement was more pronounced: visits to foster households were more frequent and the broader emphasis adopted in such cases was illustrated by the greater efforts made in working with the child's family.

Despite these important differences, however, several of our findings have been remarkably consistent throughout this study. We have seen that the County Authority has had the dubious distinction of possessing the highest placement breakdown level in each of the three fostering categories examined. As before, and in contrast to earlier studies in this area, we discovered no relationship between the early separation of children from families and future placement outcome. However, as we have discovered throughout this study, fostering breakdown is associated with a longer care career and the situation of the long-stay care population gives particular cause for concern. It was also revealed that the separation and isolation in care of siblings is associated with placement failure although – in contrast to earlier evidence – findings concerning discontinuity in schooling and the significance of unrelated foster children were inconclusive. Finally, the importance of certain placement-related factors was also reaffirmed: the preparatory training of foster parents was found to be rewarded with greater stability, while the problem of perceived competition with foster parents' own children persists.

Notes

1   See J. Rowe, *Fostering in the Eighties*, British Agencies for Adoption and Fostering, 1983; J. Triseliotis ed., *New Developments in Foster Care and Adoption*, Routledge and Kegan Paul, 1980.
2   Department of the Environment, *The Provision of Child Care: A Study at Eight Local Authorities in England and Wales*, Department of the Environment, 1981; M. Knapp, A. Fenyo and E. Robertson, *Children in Care: Progress on Costs and Efficiency*, memorandum submitted to the Social Services Commitee of the House of Commons, Personal Social Services Research Unit, University of Kent, 1986; M. Knapp, 'Children in care: planning without costs', in Nuffield/York portfolio no. 1, 1985. See also J. Thoburn, A. Murdoch and A. O'Brien, *Permanence in Child Care*, Basil Blackwell, 1986.
3   A useful overview is provided in N. Hazel, *A Bridge to Independence: The Kent Family Placement Project*, Basil Blackwell, 1981.
4   M. Shaw and T. Hipgrave, *Specialist Fostering*, Batsford, 1983.
5   A. Keefe, *Foster Care: A Research Study on the NCH Project in Gloucester and Avon*, National Children's Home, 1983.
6   J. Thomas, *Survey of Special Fostering Schemes in London*, London Boroughs' Children's Regional Planning Committee, 1982.
7   M. Yelloly, *Independent Evaluation of Twenty-Five Placements (Kent Family Placement Project)*, Kent Social Services Department, 1979.
8   See chapter 1.
9   M. Stein and K. Carey, *Leaving Care*, Basil Blackwell, 1986.
10   See D. Berridge, *Children's Homes*, Basil Blackwell, 1985.

8

Findings from the Intensive Study

In this chapter we discuss findings arising from the detailed-examination of a small number of foster placements in which breakdown occurred. Readers will recall that material from this intensive study has already been presented in chapters 3 and 5 in the form of two case studies – Paul and Shirley. In these chapters, we saw the way in which findings from our extensive survey operated in specific instances: for example, the significance of social networks, peer relationships, the dynamics of the foster household and the contribution of residential care. In this chapter we now focus on the additional features perceived by participants to contribute to unsuccessful placements. We highlight the contrasting perspectives of the participants and the problems this brings. Attention will also focus on the *process* of fostering breakdown, especially the progress of the foster placement over time and developments both preceding and subsequent to the placement ending.

This chapter, therefore, concentrates on the ten placements that broke down prematurely, of which Paul and Shirley were two examples. As explained in chapter 2, the ten cases selected for intensive study were each located in the County Authority. We approached each participant who had been involved in the fosterings and eventually succeeded in interviewing ten social workers, another five social workers who had been allocated to work with the foster parents, seven natural parents, eight residential workers, seven teachers and seven children. Although the ten placements chosen for the intensive investigation reflect a range of fosterings – three planned long term, three short term and four adolescents on intermediate placements – we shall in this chapter adopt a thematic approach and seek to identify a number of common features of these unsuccessful placements.

At this stage, a word of caution is necessary as it is important to stress that the ten placements selected are unlikely to constitute a typical group of fosterings, insofar as they each eventually ran into serious difficulty. Furthermore, the common features that we identify are not necessarily restricted to unsuccessful placements alone. Nevertheless, we shall seek to identify broad themes of the unsuccessful placements investicated, in particular the causes and effects of breakdown.

Before commencing our intensive analysis, it is first helpful to refer briefly to a particularly relevant recent research study. As part of a broader investigation, Aldgate and Hawley interviewed members of 11 foster households who had been involved in placement breakdowns.[1] It is interesting to note that a number of their findings echo those of our own study; we shall, therefore, list their main conclusions. Initially, Aldate and Hawley discovered that what were termed 'disruptions' were highly significant events for households and they arose as a result of a cumulative process. The decision to 'disrupt' was found not to have been taken lightly; indeed, foster families were discovered to have suffered emotionally and the residue of feelings had often been left unresolved. Aldgate and Hawley highlighted five main causes of 'disruption': first, was the children's behaviour; second, foster children's inability to demonstrate sufficient attachment to families; third, these problems were often aggravated by foster parents' own personal and family problems; fourth, was the ill-defined access of natural parents; and, finally, the removal of the child was felt to be essential in order to restore the equilibrium of the foster family. It will be useful to bear in mind these points throughout this chapter, as Aldgate and Hawley reinforce a number of findings from our own study.

Features of unsuccessful placements

From the interviews that were undertaken with participants in the 10 unsuccessful placements in our intensive study, seven broad themes can be identified. Each of these are discussed below. In summary, they are: the complex nature of the breakdown process; the way in which placement endings are negotiated; contrasting expectations of placements; the isolation of foster parents; the exclusion of natural parents; poor co-ordination of services; and, finally, resource difficulties.

The complex nature of the breakdown process

In general, as has also been found to occur in the natural families of children admitted to care,[2] it was apparent that the deterioration of placements tended to occur over a period of some months and as a result of a complex series of events. In none of the ten fosterings was the breakdown precipitated by a *single* major crisis. There was often, however, an occurrence, of no particular significance in itself and often – as foster parents frequently conceded – quite trivial, which led to the placement entering a final, decisive phase. Naturally, in our earlier categorization of the reasons for placement breakdowns, we were careful not to assume that such events – which were often described in social workers' records in elaborate detail – were the sole precipitating factor. For example, following a family argument, a boy in a planned long-stay placement climbed a tree and, despite a variety of exhortations and threats, remained there for two hours. Another youth refused to dress in a particular way for a job interview; while a girl in an intermediate placement rearranged her bedroom furniture contrary to the wishes of her foster parents. Clearly, one would not expect such events to herald major crises and foster parents had previously dealt with similar problems on numerous occasions. Yet, as a culmination of a long period of stress, a stubborn act of defiance often led a foster parent to telephone a social worker to insist upon the removal of the child.

Although, as one would expect, the quality of experience that they were able to offer varied, it was nevertheless apparent from interviews that, almost without exception, families had gone to considerable lengths to accommodate their foster children. A gradual wearing-down process had occurred and, eventually, foster children had totally dominated family life. One foster mother expressed this as follows:

He was all we ever talked about – our complete lives were taken over by that kid. He just became the complete centre of attention and our own two were forgotten. Month after month – my husband, John, was away at work of course – I had him all through the school holidays and he just drained me until I had nothing left to give. He just took over everything. I had no idea it would be as bad as that.

This gradual debilitation was particularly noticeable in two of the planned short-stay placements which were significantly prolonged. In both cases, foster parents described in painful detail the tensions that had arisen between themselves and social workers while the children in their care, who had been expected to stay only weeks, had remained many months. The difficulties inherent in providing short-term fostering for young children were graphically described; particularly the problem of providing high quality care without becoming too emotionally attached to a child who could depart at short notice. Thus, short-term foster parents might deliberately delay the onset of important developmental stages – such as toilet training – as it was perceived that difficulties could ensue if the process was interrupted on children being moved. Short-term foster parents identified this enforced detachment as a particular source of stress and one that led to considerable conflicts with social workers.

The negotiation of placement endings

An interesting second finding, particularly concerning the four adolescents in our intensive sample who had been living in a variety of intermediate placements, was that there was a process of *negotiation* surrounding the ending of placements. 'Breakdown' was not a final, decisive act. Instead in each case, once serious difficulties set in, the status of the placement was renegotiated by participants. Social worker involvement could be crucial at this phase but was not always forthcoming.

Two examples illustrate this process of negotiation. In one case a 14-year old youth, Nick, was placed on a specialist fostering scheme with experienced foster parents. After a year, friction between Nick and his foster mother became serious. Following a heated argument one day, she telephoned his social worker and informed him that family life was rapidly becoming intolerable. However, the social worker responsible for the case was absent on holiday and his duty social work colleague responded by removing Nick the following day to a residential home; whether this was intended to be a temporary or a permanent remedy is unclear. On returning from his well-earned leave, the social worker was furious that this carefully nurtured placement had been jeopardized. In interview, he insisted that similar problems had previously occurred and that if he had not been absent, the foster family would have remained intact. Despite working hard over the following three months at a reconciliation, Nick adamantly refused to return. When interviewed, the youth explained his actions in the following manner:

I suppose looking back I was stupid not to go back to them. They gave me a good home and I was just being stubborn. If Dilip hadn't been away on holiday at the time he'd probably have talked me out of it like he always did. But I also thought that they deserved a rest from me. I'd put them through hell and they were both getting on a bit so it was probably best that I went.

A second example of the way in which placement endings were subject to negotiation concerned Gordon, who was 16. Gordon was attending a Youth Training Scheme and, one day, his group were to rehearse interview techniques. That morning over breakfast, Gordon informed his mother that he was being interviewed. The latter, unfamiliar with the subtleties of 'role play' hastily ironed a shirt and fetched a tie. Gordon failed to convince his foster mother that this was unnecessary and insisted on wearing his favourite T shirt, which had been torn with meticulous detail. A row erupted, both parties gave vent to feelings which they subsequently regretted and Gordon stormed from the house, claiming that he would never return but instead would move in with his sister. However, Gordon did return at midnight the same evening, on the pretence that he was collecting some of his clothes. During interview, Gordon stated that he had wanted to remain with his foster parents but had been unable to express the necessary request. Similarly, his foster parents remarked that they had wanted him to remain but did not say so. Only afterwards had Gordon's social worker been informed of these events.

These two brief illustrations demonstrate the negotiations that often surround placement endings. Of course, it *may* be wholly appropriate and to the benefit of all that placements such as these come to an end. However interviews revealed that, in retrospect, participants not infrequently regretted their decisions and timely interventions by social workers may have led to a quite different course of events.

Contrasting expectations of foster placements

A third, particularly noticeable, feature of these ten unsuccessful fosterings was that participants often had contrasting

– indeed, sometimes contradictory – expectations of placements. For example, as we described earlier, two of the
three 'short-term' placements were expected by foster
parents to last a matter of weeks, yet endured for a year and
a year-and-a-half respectively. Clearly, if such a mismatch of
perceptions exists, the intentions of one or other party are
quite likely to be thwarted.

It is obviously desirable for substitute arrangements to be
responsive to changing circumstances. Yet it was disconcerting to discover in a number of the placements that social
workers admitted that they had not been wholly truthful
with foster parents: when confronted, three of them
affirmed that the foster parents had been deceived or even
manipulated. One social worker rationalized this as follows:

> Yes, I admit it, you're right. I conned them. As a result, we lost a
> good foster home and their marriage nearly split up. But what else
> could I have done? I wanted good foster parents for those girls and
> they were the best going. I kept hoping that things would work out
> all right and they didn't – I was wrong. It preys on my mind what I
> did to that family, don't you worry.

The outset of a foster placement is obviously an important
phase in which to clarify objectives. But the circumstances in
which several of the placements were initiated would appear
far from satisfactory and did not follow general, official
guidelines.[3] For example Gordon, discussed earlier, had
originally visited his foster parents only during holiday
periods. However, on departing from his CHE during the
summer of his 16th birthday, he simply remained at the
foster home. Both Gordon and his foster parents were,
initially at least, satisfied with this arrangement. Yet the
placement seems to have arisen, as Gordon's social worker
admitted, without the conscious approval of the Social
Services Department.

The origins of some other placements in our intensive
study were equally unconvincing. One couple, who had
applied to the Department to act as long-term foster parents
for a young child, were persuaded instead, against their

better judgement, to accept an adolescent girl on an intermediate basis. It was also common for foster parents (as with a number of teachers that we interviewed) to be provided with remarkably little, if any, information concerning their foster children – illustrating their powerlessness. One couple, for example, remained ignorant of the fact that a child's father had hanged himself. Consequently, a number of myths tended to build up concerning natural parents' behaviour – often involving misuse of alcohol and aggression. In the absence of more accurate information, these prejudices at least partially explain the reluctance of a number of foster parents to encourage contact between children and natural parents.

The isolation of foster parents

A fourth marked characteristic of our sample of fostering breakdowns was the isolation of foster parents from social work support. It was exceptional for foster parents to be invited to contribute regularly to case reviews; for example, two couples who respectively had been fostering for nine and six years not only had never been invited to reviews but were even unaware that such machinery existed.

It was rare, therefore, for foster parents and social workers to communicate freely. One foster mother, who had participated in a specialist fostering scheme for particularly demanding children, had wrongly perceived that the enhanced payments she and her husband received implied that they should be independent in the care of the child; a form of sub-contracting, almost. Another foster mother replied, pertinently, 'I wouldn't want to *pester* the social worker'. Consequently, it was not unexpected that, when foster parents were asked whom they would first contact concerning serious child care problems, the majority view was that they would initially seek guidance from other foster parents or their extended family, rather than the social services.

The main reason for the lack of support to foster placements was that social workers chose to restrict their involve-

ment. Most of the foster parents who were interviewed
stated that social workers would only visit them if they were
requested to do so; or if a placement was experiencing
particular problems. They were then felt to be highly
responsive and their input was valued. Social workers' lack
of participation in foster placements arose for a variety of
reasons. Regular support of foster households came well
down the list of priorities of most social workers. Certainly,
in the County Authority, the impression of social work we
retain from our lengthy period of fieldwork is one of 'crisis
management' – also portrayed in other studies of children in
care.[4] One social worker claimed that, of her existing
caseload of 30, there were 13 cases of child abuse. She
added: 'I go to sleep at night literally with my fingers
crossed, worrying about some of those cases. Unless I've got
a strong indication that something's seriously wrong, a
fostering's the least of my worries.'

Another reason for the lack of social worker participation
in foster placements was that it was sometimes perceived
that involvement would be unwelcome. An advantage of our
approach to the intensive study was that it enabled us to
examine assertions such as these by questioning different
parties. Social workers commonly stated that they felt
uneasy when visiting the foster homes and suspected that
their participation was unwelcome. These did not seem to be
later rationalizations of an unsatisfactory state of affairs. Yet
when we interviewed foster parents, including those whose
social workers had expressed greatest unease, they certainly
did not reinforce this view and would have preferred, they
claimed, greater social work involvement. Thus, a degree of
incongruence had developed between social workers' and
foster parents' perspectives, which had undermined the
progress of placements.

The exclusion of natural parents

We have observed from earlier chapters that the exclusion of
natural parents is not only a feature of unsuccessful place-

ments but typifies fosterings more generally. Nevertheless, a fifth major theme evident from our more detailed scrutiny of the 10 placements was that the role of natural parents was a source of considerable conflict. Despite wishing to maintain regular involvement, natural parents sometimes were not provided with the address of the foster household but, instead, had to meet on neutral territory. These restrictions were particularly puzzling to certain parents as, either prior or subsequent to the fostering, their children had lived in residential establishments which, rightly or wrongly, pursued policies of unrestricted access. Shirley's situation, described in chapter 5, was an example of this. As one natural mother put it:

I didn't know where I was. One month they were telling me to come and see her night and day and then she moved to that foster home and I could only see her every other week down at social services. And the plan was still for her to come back to me when I got things sorted out. You don't wonder why some people give up.

Our interviews also revealed a degree of misunderstanding over the reasons for restricting natural parents' access to their children. As was shown earlier in this chapter, foster parents were supplied with sparse information on children's backgrounds and often held inaccurate images of natural parents. In all but one of the placements in which the role of natural parents was particularly problematic, social workers justified their restrictive policies in terms of *foster parents'* unease concerning access. However, when foster couples were then interviewed, we seldom perceived there to be this degree of antipathy. Instead, the absence of parental contact was explained as the *social worker's* preference.

We do not claim that a single interview can provide a full understanding of the complexities of a case. Furthermore, we appreciate that what people report and how they act are not always synonymous. Nevertheless, our interviews once again highlighted the different perceptions of social workers and foster parents. Under appropriate circumstances, and with adequate encouragement and professional support, our findings indicate that foster parents may be more 'inclusive' of parental participation than is often believed.

Poor co-ordination of services

A sixth theme emerging from our interviews with participants in unsuccessful fosterings was the poor co-ordination of services. Again, we would not be so naive as to suggest that, in placements that do not break down, inter-agency planning is exemplary. Yet it was clear that the existing problems in foster placements were sometimes compounded by the absence of effective co-operation between services.

For example Nick, introduced earlier in this chapter, was fostered in a rural area which was served by one large comprehensive school. When interviewed, his former head of year stated that, for the first six months at his new school, Nick made good progress but he eventually adopted the role of 'classroom joker'. One morning, due to his misbehaviour, Nick was awarded a detention. He was called by his teacher to the front of the classroom and given a detention slip – which he proceeded to eat. Nick was subsequently expelled from school and, despite the efforts of his social worker, received no education for eight weeks of the winter term. This also meant that he spent considerable periods of time at home with his foster mother which, according to his social worker, led to additional stress. Nick's former head of year affirmed that the former pupil was excluded from school for what were trivial incidents and, knowing of the problems in his domestic circumstances, his school should have made a greater effort.

Similar problems emerged concerning an adolescent girl on an intermediate foster placement, who was due to commence a Manpower Services Commission course to coincide with her arrival at the foster home. Owing to bureaucratic delay, her starting date for the course was postponed for three months, which meant that much time was spent at the foster home unoccupied.

Especially for adolescents in care, a foster placement was often one of a package of services intended to alleviate problems. As we have seen, foster placements could be jeopardized if part of the package was not delivered – whether it be schooling, vocational training or problems over Social Security. Increased sensitivity on the part of other agencies, and greater awareness on the part of social workers of the significance of complementary services, may have enabled some foster placements better to withstand other pressures.

Resource difficulties

A final point relevant to the progress of foster placements concerns resource difficulties. We were repeatedly struck by the problems confronting social workers when trying to locate suitable placements. These problems were particularly acute concerning adolescents. Consequently, social workers frequently remarked that, from the outset, they had strong reservations about the viability of placements, yet few alternatives existed. Hence, as we have already seen, one couple who had intended as an initial placement to foster a young child was instead persuaded to accept an adolescent girl. Moreover Gordon, on leaving his CHE at 16, simply remained in his holiday foster placement.

As was demonstrated in chapter 4, a lasting impression that we have a fostering services is the significance of 'supply-side' factors. Despite the rhetoric of assessment for children in care and the concept of 'individualized treatment', children clearly received what was available. For certain groups of children – including adolescents and those who had previously failed in foster homes – in the County Authority at least, options were severely limited. Thus, 'marginal' fosterings were sometimes pursued; these often proved to be unsatisfactory.

The effects of fostering breakdown

Our intensive study of ten unsuccessful placements also provided us with the opportunity to explore the effects of fostering breakdowns – primarily on children but also on other participants. In our extensive, retrospective study of social workers' records – described in chapters 4, 6 and 7 – we also gathered useful information on social workers' perceptions of placement endings. However, this area is more satisfactorily investigated by focusing in detail on individual placements and by exploring contrasting perceptions of circumstances surrounding placement breakdown.

Notwithstanding the above, our wider statistical analysis led to a number of valuable insights into the effects of the termination of foster placements. In particular, it revealed that – as with factors precipitating breakdown – the effects of unsuccessful placements, particularly on children's development, are highly complex.

This finding was reinforced in our intensive study and the effects of fostering breakdown on children are by no means unidimensional. Some children, in the immediate aftermath, were highly distressed and this was reflected in violent behaviour, delinquent acts, depression or deep withdrawal. As one youth explained when interviewed:

I just went to pieces after I left the Gibsons. I really trusted that couple. The thing that hurt me most was that I thought it was going dead good and then they suddenly turned round and said they'd changed their minds and didn't want to foster. I really went mad when I got to Shorelands. I never realized I had a temper like that before and it all came out, and I just wanted to destroy everything. My world had fell apart.

Yet equal numbers of children, although being initially subdued, revealed – at least superficially – no major signs of dejection. In fact, some were clearly relieved to depart from placements in which their needs and wishes had remained unfulfilled. A small number of children were reported by social workers immediately to have flourished in subsequent placements. Also, children's educational performance did not necessarily deteriorate. Thus, the effects of placement endings on children are complex. Some children in the face of adversity displayed remarkable resilience; others suffered profoundly. It is also important to differentiate between short-term symptoms of discontinuity and the longer-term erosion of trust, which undoubtedly occurs.

It would have been rather ambitious in a study of this nature to attempt to ascertain why the experience of fostering breakdown produced a differential response. Numerous variables would have had to be considered and it was apparent that, alongside the fostering experience, there were often other significant changes occurring simultaneously in children's lives. For example, one child had recently transferred from primary to secondary school prior to the fostering entering its final stages, and the natural mother of another became seriously ill. To distinguish the relative impact of these multiple changes would be fraught with difficulty, if not impossible.

It is, therefore, unwise to speculate in too much detail on why children react differently to placement termination. Clearly, various types of breakdown have different meanings; and certain children will interpret differently to others a particular event. In this respect a psychological process occurs whereby children, like others, actively redefine and recreate their social world. Hence, we uncovered no simple relationship between, for example, the effects of fostering breakdown and sex or age of children. Yet there was some suggestion of a link with two factors. First, children seemed to be more visibly distressed by the process of breakdown the longer a placement had endured. Furthermore, the effects were less noticeable for children with a longer history of separation.

The impact of fostering breakdown on children is therefore difficult, if not impossible, to establish in any objective sense. But it is interesting to note that the way different groups of adults perceived effects often contrasted sharply. This can be partially accounted for by the children's different behaviour in different contexts. Thus, by way of illustration, a child might respond differently in the presence of a social worker than when in a classroom with fellow pupils or in a residential environment. Adults occupying different roles will also be subject to different levels of exposure to a child.

Nevertheless, one important finding from the intensive study was that social workers' interpretations of the effects of termination were frequently at variance with those of other participants – residential workers, foster parents, teachers and, to a lesser degree, natural parents. Indeed, there was a much higher degree of consensus between these other groups. There were notable exceptions, such as with Nick, in which social workers were closely involved in the progress of placements. Such intimate involvement was, however, somewhat atypical; instead as we saw earlier it was more usual, perhaps inevitably, for caseworkers to adopt a more distant role. Nevertheless a consequence was that, in comparison with other professional and non-professional groups, social workers tended to underestimate the effects upon a child of a fostering breakdown. An example may help to illustrate this point.

Julie, a nine-year old, had been living in her foster placement for two-and-a-half years. She was removed at her social worker's instigation after doubts had been expressed concerning the quality of care she was receiving. We are in no position, of course, to confirm whose interpretation of Julie's subsequent adjustment was most accurate. Yet the following extracts from transcripts of interviews reveal that Julie's social worker, compared to others, had reached a quite different assessment of the situation. For example the social worker remarked:

We had a few tears the day I collected her but there's nothing unusual about that. I think she'll soon get over it. Reports from Latchmore Way are that she's settling in well and I think we can start looking pretty soon for another foster situation. The last thing we want is for her to become institutionalized.

Her 'key-worker' at the children's home, however, observed:

There is no doubt about it but that fostering breaking down has done her untold damage. She's only now started to open up a bit with me about what it meant to her. We've got a long way to go with her before she's ready for another family and if her social worker thinks that, then she'd better think again.

Comments from Julie's teacher also suggested that her recent unsettled experienced had had a profound effect on her performance and behaviour at school:

She's a different child completely now than she was before the fostering breakdown and her emotional insecurity gets in the way of her learning. She was always a popular girl in her class but now she is much more distant in her relationships with her friends as well as with me. I've also found her on her own crying in the playground more than once. She's much less confident about things than she used to be before the recent changes.

Some difference in perceptions no doubt stems from contrasting professional backgrounds and ideologies. However, regardless of its origins, it was noticeable from our interviews that social workers approached the aftermath of a failed fostering rather differently to other professional groups. As a result, disagreements could occur regarding the timing and nature of future plans. Obviously, when decision-making occurs, social workers receive various inputs from colleagues working in different contexts. The role of the social worker is, however, central and it is she or he who will exert the greatest influence.

Effects on foster parents

When considering the impact of fostering breakdown, however, we should not be led to believe that it is only foster children who are adversely affected by the experience. Our series of interviews also revealed that, in the majority of cases, foster parents were also deeply affected by preceding events and the removal of the child. This was clearly apparent regarding Paul's placement, described in chapter 3. In retrospect, most foster couples did not regret the placement ending when it did. But this did little to minimize the stress resulting from the combination of exasperation and guilt. Of the ten foster couples, four foster mothers and two foster fathers wept during interviews. Some couples claimed that the episode had almost led to the partners' separation. One foster mother experienced what was diagnosed as a nervous breakdown, and another resorted to a course of tranquillizers. In the final throes of one placement, the foster parents' own children – and their suffering was not unusual – had requested that they be allowed to move to live with their grandparents. Several interviewees were haunted by powerful, recurring images of their former foster children, for example: 'I'll never forget his little face looking back at me through that car window as he drove off.'

With few exceptions, foster parents had indisputably made considerable investments in their relationships with children. Despite the face that several couples had seen many children come and go, their sense of loss remained significant and most foster parents who were interviewed held themselves – usually unjustifiably – responsible for the downfall of the placement.

In view of the amount of suffering by foster parents, it was particularly disquieting to discover that, overall, little effort was invested by the host agency in assisting foster parents to come to terms with their painful experiences. Consequently, four couples have since vowed that they will never again foster – and have kept to their word. One pair alleged that shortly afterwards they received a letter, with no accompanying explanation and not followed-up by a visit from a social worker, informing them that they would not be considered for a further placement. It was described earlier how a number of social workers admitted that they had not been wholly truthful with foster parents in their description of intended plans. Furthermore, we discovered that it was not uncommon for minimal information to be conveyed regarding foster children. And despite the considerable suffering experienced by a number of foster parents, we found that the Departmental response lacked sensitivity. We do not wish to stray too far from the stance of disinterested researchers. Faced with such findings, however, it is difficult to come to a conclusion other than that – regardless of whether social workers felt that alternatives existed – some foster families in our intensive sample were exploited.

Our intensive study is not, however, cause for despair. Although, according to our definition, each of the ten placements broke down, this does not necessarily imply that contact between children and former foster parents abruptly ceased. In fact in several of the placements, each involving older children, the relationship has continued in some form: Paul, introduced in chapter 3, still refers to his former carers as 'my foster parents'; two children continue to visit their previous foster parents at regular intervals; and two others are in frequent contact by telephone. In interviews with these older children and their former foster parents, this continuing contact was felt to be mutually beneficial.

Nevertheless our interviews with social workers, confirmed by our extensive investigation, discovered that caseworkers are often uneasy about continued contact with former foster parents. This reflects the 'all or nothing' attitude, highlighted in other research, in which care careers are often viewed by social workers as a set of discrete packages rather than an integrated experience.[5] Continued contact with natural parents is often discouraged (or not encouraged) for similar reasons. However, as we have stated elsewhere, there is evidence – particularly for older children – that a configuration of relationships can be satisfactorily negotiated with a variety of adult figures, so long as the roles occupied by each do not become confused.[6] Thus, with children's agreement – and it will obviously not be appropriate in all circumsttances – we do not see why relationships with former foster parents should not be nurtured. Indeed, our evidence from the intensive study suggests that children can benefit considerably when carers continue to demonstrate an interest in their welfare.

Longer-term effects

We now conclude our empirical analysis by taking a slightly longer-term view of the ten children featured in our intensive study. This brief follow-up focuses, in most instances, on children some 18 months after the foster breakdown occurred. As we shall see it reveals that, despite the earlier setbacks in planning, many cases – depending on individual judgement – were proceeding more satisfactorily. Two younger children and a pair of siblings had since been adopted, reflecting an interesting change in emphasis and a greater focus on 'permanency planning'.[7] Shirley (see chapter 5) has now returned home and is making good progress at school. Her position at home, however, was described with some justification by her social worker as 'precarious', although she had been living with her parents for a year and there were grounds for encouragement. Paul, introduced in chapter 3, is still living in the residential home in which we left him. He has found it extremely difficult to come to terms with his mother's death and his fostering experience is reported to have seriously undermined his self-confidence. Nevertheless, more structured contact between Paul and his father has been built up and their ultimate reunion remains the social worker's long-term strategy.

Of the five other children in our intensive sample, one boy, following widespread national advertising and prolonged debates over financial dispensation, has been carefully introduced to another planned long-term foster family as an 'out of county' placement. An adolescent girl, following a lengthy residential interlude, had recently moved to a 'special fostering placement', as part of a new scheme for 'difficult to place' children which the County Authority is seeking to expand. Another boy has unfortunately been subject to a *further* fostering breakdown, due to a combination of the behavioural problems he was posing and his social worker's concern about the quality of experience with which he was being provided.

The final two cases in our intensive study are the two youths whom we met earlier in this chapter, Nick and Gordon. Having exhausted virtually all social services provision in the county, in addition to a mixed economy of voluntary and independent residential facilities – indeed, he claims during his life in 'care' to have been moved twenty times – Nick is now accommodated in a hostel managed by the Probation Service. Owing, perhaps, to a curious oversight on his part, Nick has no record of criminality but he is reported by his social worker to be responding well to the blend of structure and independence which he is being offered. An added bonus of this enlightened institutional experience is that the Probation Service has negotiated a collaborative arrangement with a local housing association, whereby certain residents can be provided with a self-contained flat. In six months' time, Nick is thus due for his 21st move but one of the few that he has welcomed.

We can see, therefore, that all is not necessarily gloom and doom and several of our ten initially unsuccessful cases appear to have discovered a period of stability. The same cannot be said of Gordon. Following his departure from CHE, he remained by default in his holiday foster placement until it came to an uncertain ending. He then lived with an assortment of acquaintances in a series of unsatisfactory, temporary arrangements. Eventually, in an effort hopefully to contain Gordon in the year preceding his rather undignified exit from care on his 18th birthday, he was provided by his social worker with a typed list of the names and addresses of establishments offering board and lodging accommodation. In what was clearly a sociologically functional if, perhaps, irresponsible act of anticipatory socialization, he thus joined the nomadic hordes of the homeless. Gordon proceeded through the list with a degree of alacrity and, within an eight-month period, had briefly sampled no fewer than 12 of the 20 addresses with which he was initially presented.

As only limited research has been undertaken into the problems associated with departure from care, it is perhaps premature to comment.[8] Nevertheless, from the little information that is available, it is possible that the quite major problems surrounding foster care that we have highlighted in this book are overshadowed by the deficiencies in services for young adults who leave the care system.

Conclusion

In this chapter we have examined in detail, by interviewing a range of participants, ten foster placements in which premature breakdown occurred. We would again urge caution in extrapolating to a broader group of fosterings from this intensive sample. For reasons explained in chapter 2, the ten placements selected for detailed study were each located in the County Authority. Furthermore, it would be unwise to deduce that, by avoiding some of the pitfalls identified in this chapter, the number of unsuccessful fosterings would automatically be reduced. Against all odds, some fosterings no doubt survive in spite of the many problems that we have discussed; others can flounder for no apparent reason.

Yet as the common themes that we have outlined were identified by participants – particularly foster parents and social workers – as exacerbating the problems that *already* existed in placements, it would seem reasonable to assume that some attention paid to these areas would be expected to ameliorate problems. Thus, the contrasting perspectives highlighted in this intensive study complement the earlier, extensive analysis. It has also yielded insights into the *process* of fostering breakdown, particularly its causes and effects.

More specifically, seven broad themes stood out from our interviews with participants in the ten unsuccessful placements. It is noticeable that there was a high level of consensus between our findings and those of Aldgate and Hawley, introduced at the beginning of this chapter.[9] Initially we discovered that the deterioration of fosterings was an immensely complex process. Second, and leading on from this, a pertinent finding was that placement endings are often preceded by a period of elaborate negotiation; and that certain inputs – including a timely contribution from a social worker – could profoundly influence the outcome. A third noticeable feature of our intensive study was the extent to which participants often had contrasting, and even sometimes contradictory, expectations. Fourth were the problems accruing from the isolation of foster parents from social work support. A fifth theme concerned the difficulties associated with the exclusion of natural parents from foster placements. Sixth was the poor co-ordination of services. While, finally, a feature of the ten unsuccessful placements studied was resource difficulties.

We also explored the implications of fostering breakdown and, once again, discovered that the effects on participants are far from straightforward. Thus, some children would be highly, visibly distressed at a placement termination; others, superficially at least, appeared to cope rather better. Nonetheless, it was interesting to observe that the *perceived* effects of breakdown often contrasted sharply between different groups. In particular, whether because of the particular role they adopted, professional ideology, or a consequence of the stoicism resulting from the essentially 'crisis-management' nature of their work,[10] social workers tended to underestimate the effects of fostering breakdown in comparison with other professional groups.

It was also found that the effects of a placement termination on foster parents are often profound. Moreover, Departmental responses to these problems sometimes lacked sensitivity.

We saw in chapters 3 and 5 from our detailed inspection of two of our case studies – Paul and Shirley – the way in which findings from our extensive study operated in specific instances. In this chapter, we have identified additional features contributing to placement breakdown. In the concluding chapter we shall combine findings from our extensive and intensive studies and consider the implications of this research for the organization and delivery of foster care.

Notes

1   J. Aldgate and D. Hawley, 'Helping foster families through disruption', *Adoption and Fostering*, vol. 10, no. 2, 1986, pp. 44–9.
2   M. Fisher, P. Marsh, D. Phillips and E. Sainsbury, *In and Out of Care: The Experiences of Children, Parents and Social Workers*, Batsford, 1986; J. Packman, J. Randall, N. Jacques, *Who Needs Care?*, Basil Blackwell, 1986.
3   For example Department of Health and Social Security, Scottish Office, Scottish Education Department, Social Work Services Group and Welsh Office, *Guide to Fostering Practice*, HMSO, 1976.
4   See J. Vernon and D. Fruin, *In Care: A Study of Social Work Decision Making*, National Children's Bureau, 1986; Department of Health and Social Security, *Social Work Decisions in Child Care: Recent Research Findings and their Implications*, HMSO, 1985.
5   D. Berridge, *Children's Homes*, Basil Blackwell, 1985.
6   Ibid.
7   J. Vernon, *Developments in Planning for Children in Care*, National Children's Bureau, 1986.
8   An important exception is M. Stein and K. Carey, *Leaving Care*, Basil Blackwell, 1986.
9   J. Aldgate and D. Hawley, 'Helping foster families through disruption'.
10 S. Millham, R. Bullock, K. Hosie and M. Haak, *Lost in Care: The Problems of Maintaining Links Between Children in Care and their Families*, Gower, 1986; Packman et al., *Who Needs Care?*

9

Conclusion

Having analysed our research finding on long-, short-term and intermediate fostering, and incorporated material from both extensive and intensive studies, we shall now bring together some of the main themes arising from this investigation and make some general observations.

An important point that should be stressed is that we have discovered a number of encouraging findings. For example, most foster placements were found to have proceeded satisfactorily. Breakdown rates in two of the three agencies that were studied were lower than many observers would have anticipated and, in particular, there are grounds for optimism regarding short-term and intermediate placements. Furthermore, many placements that were unsuccessful in terms of duration were found, nevertheless, to have had a number of positive influences. And in placements that failed, contact between foster parents and children often continued and was an important factor. Therefore, in seeking to identify and thus, hopefully, rectify the deficiencies of foster care, we should not become over-pessimistic.

Our results, on the other hand, give few grounds for complacency. Particularly as foster care continues to become an increasingly popular option for children in care, a number of findings are disquieting – certainly in one of the agencies studied. For example, we should remind ourselves that, in the County Authority, two in every five planned long-term fosterings were terminated within three years; and over a third of intermediate placements were doomed within twelve months. No doubt some critics will claim that practice has improved markedly since the research fieldwork was conducted. We should remind ourselves, however, that there was no evidence that the incidence of unsuccessful fosterings had declined in recent years, suggesting an intriguing degree of long-term continuity.[1] Our investigation also unearthed its fair share of particularly worrying individual episodes; no more but, certainly, no fewer than in our previous study of residential child care contexts.[2] A number of our findings, therefore, should encourage serious thought about the quality of experience provided in substitute families.

Agency comparisons

It is necessary at this stage to return to the issue of comparative breakdown rates between our study agencies. The level of unsuccessful placements was consistently higher in the County Authority than elsewhere. Indeed, although it is a subject that we were unable to explore in detail, it is pertinent to note that the County Authority continues to foster a larger proportion of children in its care than does the London Borough (two-thirds compared to half); it may be, therefore, that the former utilizes more 'marginal' placements.

We explained at the outset that the two Social Services Departments involved in this research favoured contrasting approaches towards the organization of foster care. In particular, the London Borough had developed a more specialist, centralized service. Although our study was essentially a child-centred one and we were unable to explore in detail organizational factors, our extensive analysis did enable us to observe whether differences in outcome could be attributed wholly to child-, family-, and placement-related variables, or whether there were other, unexplained, significant differences associated with Departments' policies and practice.

Our study of short-term fostering revealed only a slight difference in breakdown rates between the two Social Services Departments and so this particular area will not be pursued. In planned long-term placements, however, a considerable difference was apparent. Yet, on detailed examination, it was discovered that variation in outcomes could be attributed primarily to the case-related criteria that we explored and that, in itself, for example, the more specialist approach towards fostering favoured by the one agency was not a significant, explanatory factor. Instead, the London Borough and the County Authority revealed contrasting child populations in long-term fostering. This was, nevertheless, at least partially attributable to the policy of the London Borough regarding the more selective use of traditional, open-ended fostering, particularly for older children; and the greater incidence of structured, intermediate placements. The particular practices of the London Borough that distinguished it from the County Authority and led, in turn, to fewer, long-term fostering failures were essentially twofold: first, a greater preference for voluntary rather than compulsory care arrangements (which to some extent, but not entirely, is age-related); and, secondly, a more open – or 'inclusive' – approach towards fostering, demonstrated in increased levels of contact between children and natural parents, and between the latter and social workers.

Similar factors account for differing degrees of success in intermediate placements. In the County Authority, those placements that we categorized as 'intermediate' consisted virtually entirely of adolescents placed on a 'specialist fostering scheme', with foster parents receiving enhanced payments. In the London Borough and the Voluntary Agency, in contrast, younger children were also accommodated, including both those with and without 'special needs'.

As we saw, breakdown rates in intermediate fostering were related to age (older children were more likely to experience unsuccessful placements); differences in the level of success between agencies, therefore, can to some degree be attributed to this age composition.

Other criteria accounting for the variation in placement stability in intermediate fostering between agencies are, as with long-term placements, essentially twofold: greater parental involvement, and a higher degree of social worker activity, both with natural families and foster households. In contrast to the County Authority, these practices were noticeably more common in the London Borough and placements arranged by the Voluntary Agency. Nevertheless, our analysis revealed that differences in outcome of intermediate placements are not wholly attributable to the factors that we have so far identified – that is, age of children, and parental and social worker involvement. Instead, there are also unexplained, agency-related factors that are relevant. We were unable in a study of this nature to explore this in any rigorous manner; it would, therefore, be unwise to speculate. Nevertheless, it was clear in intermediate fostering that there were differences between the three agencies with regard, for example, to the selection of foster parents; case-review; and the support offered to – and also, very importantly, between – foster parents. Although we were unable to assess their impact, it would be surprising if such contrasting practices were not reflected to a degree in placement outcomes.

Perspectives guiding the analysis

In exploring the factors associated with 'failure' and 'success' in foster care, we feel that the three perspectives that we developed in our 'extensive' analysis – characteristics and early rearing history of children, children's social networks and 'placement-related' factors – were a useful means of approaching this subject and organizing the analysis of data.

The three types of fostering that we have considered in this study, as we have shown, clearly differ in a number of important respects. Yet despite this, there is a surprising degree of congruence in our results. For example, in each type of fostering, the attempt to relate placement outcome to biographical factors and early care history was largely unproductive. There was some evidence of a link between age of children and placement failure but the relationship was not as pronounced as one might have expected from other research. Instead, particularly with planned long-term fostering, the experience of placement failure was rather more evenly distributed across age-groups. The situation of 'middle-age' or 'latency' children – the six to elevens – is especially disconcerting and we would emphasize, on the basis of our results, that fostering breakdown is not the sole prerogative of adolescents.

If child-related factors were mostly unrewarding in helping to pinpoint successful placements, the management of children's care careers and social networks were more significant. In general, the degree of effort invested in introducing a child to a foster home was a useful indicator of likely outcome. While particularly in long-term (but *not* short-term) placements, an interlude of some months prior to fostering in a more neutral, residential environment was found to be positively associated with successful placements. Overall, the role of natural parents was also an important component in placement stability: fosterings tended to be more successful where contacts between children and their parents were encouraged, and where positive relationships existed between natural parents and social workers. Recent research into the child-care system has revealed how parents' involvement over time tends to wither, largely as a result of implicit barriers to contact.[3] Here, however, we have demonstrated that the withdrawal of parental interest tends to be counter-productive and is associated with placement discontinuity.

Other features pertaining to the maintenance of children's social networks have, unexpectedly, been shown to be associated with successful fostering: throughout this investigation, these factors are among those that are most consistently related to outcome. First in long-, short-, and intermediate fosterings alike, the separation of siblings between placements was found to be strongly linked with an unsettled care experience. Moreover, the significance of peers is reinforced when we consider the relationship between care career and schooling.[4] Here, readers will recall, we discovered the somewhat alarming finding that, of school-age children moving into planned long-term fosterings, no fewer than three-quarters also changed school; while of those departing from such placements, four-fifths had their education interrupted in a similar manner. It seems unrealistic to expect ill-prepared children to cope with such profound social, emotional, geographical and educational change in their lives. Indeed, as we have seen with parent and sibling relationships and schooling, when certain aspects of children's lives are held constant, change in *other* areas is more easily endured. This, admittedly, is hardly a surprising conclusion, yet it is one that seems not to have been uppermost in the minds of social workers responsible for placing all too many of the 189 children in our long-term study group.

A number of common themes, across different types of fostering, also stand out from our examination of 'placement-related' factors. Especially in planned long- and short-term placements, a disconcerting finding was that fosterings that broke down did so frequently for reasons that were largely unconnected with children's behaviour. In intermediate fosterings, however, which tended to take greater precautions over selection of suitable couples and matching with appropriate children, this was noticeably less of a problem. Other factors associated with the foster household were also closely related to outcome. For example, the importance of retaining and nurturing foster parents was highlighted by the finding that, in each type of fostering, couples with previous experience achieved significantly better results than did newcomers. As we saw in the previous chapter, however, foster parents were not always treated with sensitivity. In addition, it was encouraging to discover that – again applying to each type of fostering – foster parents who had experienced even rudimentary induction training were able to offer a greater degree of stability than those without preparation. Such basic training is becoming increasingly widespread and, on the basis of findings reported in this study, benefits might be expected not only in the quality but also continuity of the care experience.

Consistency in research findings

The dissemination and absorption into policy and practice of research findings is a complex issue.[5] Research results are not always directly translatable or even, sometimes, digestible; there is inevitably a time-lag involved in the process of infiltration; behaviour is not necessarily altered on the basis of acquiring information alone; research can relatively soon become outdated; and findings from studies of similar issues are not always in unison. We began this book by considering other research into the problem of fostering breakdown, where we discovered that what remain probably the most influential studies in this area – the works of Parker, Trasler and George – are now some 20 years old.[6] Much has changed in social policy since those days of economic expansion, the Beatles and England winning the World Cup: truly a bygone age. In social work we have seen, for example, the 1969 and 1975 legislation, the creation of Social Services Departments and the considerable growth, followed by the equally rapid curtailment, of the residential option. Clearly much has altered, both within wider society and, more specifically, the provision of social welfare.

Yet when we re-examine these three 1960s studies, which were undertaken in a quite different social context and in agencies other than our own, research findings in one major area display a quite remarkable degree of resemblance. Overall, the results of Parker, Trasler and George, it will be recalled, showed much disparity. Nevertheless, there was broad consensus concerning one issue: namely, the way in which foster placements were often jeopardized by the presence of foster parents' own children, particularly where they were either very young or of a similar age to the foster child. After a gap of some 20 years our own study, independently of other variables, has reinforced these findings – applying to short- and long-term fostering alike (numbers were insufficient to explore this factor in relation to intermediate fostering). For example, in long-term fosterings we found that, in households in which at the outset of a placement foster parents' own children under the age of five were present, 55 per cent of such placements broke down prematurely, compared with barely half this figure – 27 per cent – where such children were absent. (The comparative figures for short-term fostering were even more striking at 67 per cent and 11 per cent.) Furthermore, where foster parents' children were within five years of age of the child in our study group, failure rates were 40 per cent but 25 per cent where they were absent. (Comparable figures for short-term fostering were 53 per cent and 0 per cent.)

Although there were clearly supply difficulties in our two Social Services Departments in recruiting appropriate foster households, the degree of consistency in research results we now have in this area seems to us unequivocal. Thus, on the basis of our findings, for social workers placing children in households in which foster parents have a child of their own who is either very young or of a similar age to the foster child, the probability of success and failure is roughly the same. If we continue to place children in these circumstances, therefore, it is not because advice is unavailable but because we choose to ignore it.

Implications for the child care system

We shall bring this study to a close with some general observations on the child care system that arise from our research into the problem of fostering breakdown. Most importantly, we begin by returning to the broader context in which our research is situated. The developments described in our opening chapter, particularly the considerable expansion in foster care for children separated from their families, have continued apace since our research commenced. Certain agencies boast that no local authority children's homes now exist within their boundaries. On closer inspection, however, one often finds that the voluntary sector is required to make a residential contribution; multi-purpose 'children's centres' frequently have a small residential component; and the number of children educated in boarding special schools, particularly those catering for pupils who are ascertained as having 'emotional and behavioural' difficulties, is not insignificant. Nonetheless, the residential sector is in marked decline as, instead, increasing numbers of children in care are fostered.

On the basis of this research, we would question the wisdom of restricting options for the placement of children in care. We do not know, nationally, how many Social Services Departments resemble our County Authority in terms of placement outcomes, or whether the London Borough is more typical. However, it is clear from our wider knowledge of the field that the former is by no means exceptional. What is even more disconcerting, perhaps, is the way in which Departments not infrequently embark on particular courses of action without detailed, local information on the effectiveness of alternative services.

Following the 1960s studies of fostering breakdown, which discovered worryingly high levels of instability, the popularity of foster care diminished significantly and there was an expansion in residential resources. We would not wish to set into motion a similar course of action – our findings provide no justification for so doing. Moreover, many of the problems in our child care system stem from such 'lurching' back and forth between what should be complementary approaches. Instead, our results indicate that foster care is an appropriate intervention for some children in care but not for others; a range of different fostering styles is required; and residential care has an important role in the preparation for fostering, in dealing with the aftermath of unsuccessful family placements, and in sheltering – not necessarily indefinitely – children who cannot or will not live in another household. We hope to have provided information that is relevant to making these difficult decisions.

Our results also highlight the limitations of the traditional, open-ended, 'exclusive' approach to fostering. Rowe and her colleagues in their study of successful, long-term fostering, although questioning whether it was sufficient, revealed the valuable contribution that this service often makes.[7] We would fully endorse this view and encountered many children in similar circumstances. However, we also gained some insight into the damage inflicted on children (and foster parents) when such intervention fails.

Traditional, long-term fostering is clearly on the wane. Many, possibly most, local authorities are now pursuing a more assertive approach towards adoption if family rehabilitation proves impossible.[8] Many of the planned long-term arrangements that we studied were clearly of a 'quasi-adoptive' nature; and children who retained strong parental allegiance, as other researchers have discovered, often found this 'role ambiguity' difficult to bear.[9] It was not uncommon in our research to discover foster parents who had originally approached the Department in order to adopt but, owing to a lack of suitable children, had instead been persuaded to foster. Clearly, not all had come to appreciate the subtle role difference between the two and the expectations they had of children could lead to difficulties. We were dismayed, for example, to discover so many couples who still encourage foster children to call them 'mum' and 'dad'. Yet so long as at the outset of each placement, foster parents are required to sign a pledge undertaking 'We will look after him (sic) and bring him up as we would a child of our own',[10] our hopes are, perhaps, somewhat idealistic.

Nevertheless, our scrutiny of some 530 separate fostering experiences has led us to conclude that the assumption that damaged children can be accommodated in an 'ordinary' family environment – with a limited degree of preparation and, perhaps, four or five visits a year from a benign social worker – is frequently over-optimistic, if not naive. It would seem particularly inappropriate for children with long and complex care histories. Paradoxically, when interviewed, social workers were often in agreement with this assertion, yet continued placing children in similar environments; claiming that they would otherwise be in breach of Departmental policy and that, in any case, few alternative options were at hand.

Our research suggests that advantages would be derived if the model of 'intermediate' fostering were to be the rule rather than the exception – for children of all ages and not just adolescents. For this reason, we would question the continued use of the term 'special' as in 'special fostering scheme'. It implies that all other fostering is straightforward and unproblematic which, on the basis of our evidence, it clearly is not. Instead, it seems from examining this area in detail, that many of the problems we have identified can best begin to be tackled by ensuring that foster parents receive thorough, rather than limited or even no child care training; that expectations, and respective contributions, of participants in the fostering process need to be made explicit at the outset, to be recorded, and to be regularly reviewed; that, except in the small minority of cases where it is inappropriate, natural family involvement be welcomed and encouraged; and that intensive social work support be present. Moreover, without wishing to become embroiled in a particularly sensitive debate, it seems to us that in order both to recognize and reinforce the contribution thus outlined, foster parents should receive a more economically realistic reward for their efforts. If fostering services across the board were to be extended in this direction – which in many parts of the country has already happened – a more specialist service would develop, rather than what is sometimes still perceived as an inexpensive panacea. Indeed foster care, when costed rigorously, would probably become no less expensive than residential care and the implications of this conclusion are probably, if regrettably, as important as anything we have written so far.

Regardless of whether readers are in agreement with the above observations, it would also seem opportune for the role of foster parents within Social Services Departments to be reassessed. Neither of us were, hitherto, unfamiliar with the problems caused by demanding children. Yet an important research finding was the degree of difficulty with which many foster parents were confronted; often, by what were considered to be 'ordinary' children in care. Despite its inadequacies, we would not for a minute contemplate exchanging insecure research careers for the lot of a local authority foster parent. We would not be wholly uncritical of the quality of contribution of *some* foster parents. But as our intensive study revealed, foster parents were often bereft of professional advice and support and were sometimes subject to manipulation by social workers.

There is clearly much unrealized potential within the 70,000 or so foster parents in this country. In view of the central importance of their role within Social Services Departments, it would seem advantageous for foster parents to be accorded appropriate status – more akin to that of colleagues of social workers than clients. Again, we would repeat that such developments have occurred in some agencies, with encouraging results, but their incidence is by no means widespread. The potential perils, as well as benefits, of 'professionalization' are well known and not everyone would agree that recent changes in the working conditions of residential staff – such as reduced working hours and a tendency to live off-site – have necessarily improved the quality of service available to children.[11] It is also important not to overlook the power dimension, and it may well serve certain organizational interests for the status of foster parents to remain unaltered.

Our research into the problem of foster home breakdown, therefore, has led us to draw certain conclusions. No doubt others would wish to emphasize different messages from our analysis and we would not want to inhibit this in any way.

Regardless of interpretation, we hope that our study will encourage reflection among other researchers, policy makers, managers and practitioners on how best to provide for children who are unable to live with their own families. If so, our efforts, and those of the many people who have kindly assisted us, will have been worthwhile.

Notes

1   J. Packman, *Child Care Needs and Numbers*, Allen and Unwin, 1968; R. Parker, paper presented to University of Bristol/Dartington Social Research Unit research seminar.

2   D. Berridge, *Children's Homes*, Basil Blackwell, 1985.

3   See Department of Health and Social Security, *Social Work Decisions in Child Care: Recent Research Findings and their Implications*, HMSO, 1986.

4   See also R. Gardner, *Choice and Control in Decision Making: The Views of Young People in Care*, National Children's Bureau (forthcoming).

5   Dartington Social Research Unit, *The Dissemination of Research Findings in Social Work*, DSRU, 1983.

6   R. Parker, *Decision in Child Care*, Allen and Unwin, 1966; G. Trasler, *In Place of Parents*, Routledge and Kegan Paul, 1960; V. George, *Foster Care: Theory and Practice*, Routledge and Kegan Paul, 1970. See also chapter 1.

7   J. Rowe, H. Cain, M. Hundleby and A. Keane, *Long-Term Fostering*, Batsford, 1984.

8   J. Vernon, *Developments in Planning for Children in Care*, National Children's Bureau, 1986.

9   For example: B. Kahan, *Growing Up in Care*, Basil Blackwell, 1979; S. Loveday, *Reflections on Care*, Children's Society, 1985.

10 Statutory Instruments, 1955, no. 1377, *Children and Young Persons Boarding-Out*, HMSO, 1982, p. 14.

11 Similar developments are affecting day care services provided by childminders. See E. Ferri and D. Birchall, *Changing Childminders*, National Children's Bureau (forthcoming).

Glossary of Terms

Readers outside the UK may be unfamiliar with the following terms used in this book. Their equivalents, or explanations, are therefore provided.

Barnardo's	a charitable organization providing services for children and families.
breakdown (as in 'foster home breakdown')	disruption.
care/local authority care	legal provision whereby a local government Social Services Department can assume responsibility for children and young people under 18 with acute family and/or personal problems.
care career	a child's experience, over time, of local authority care; placement history.
care plan	case plan.

care system/child care system	child welfare system.
children's department	prior to the formation in the early 1970s of Social Services Departments (see below), children's departments were responsible in each locality for the administration of child welfare services.
Department of Health and Social Security (DHSS)	central government department with responsibility for health and social welfare programmes, incorporating social security (income support) and the personal social services (social work) as well as the National Health Service.
DHSS Social Services Inspectorate	a section of the Department of Health and Social Security, with regional branches, empowered to inspect and report on the services provided by Social Services Departments.
foster care (also traditionally referred to as 'boarding-out')	foster *family* care, *not* group/residential care.
– long-term fostering	long-term foster family care; permanent foster family care.
– short-term fostering	short-term/emergency foster family care.
– intermediate fostering	specialized foster family care; therapeutic foster family care (a 'special fostering scheme' refers to a specialized, foster family care service).
– fostering with a view to adoption	foster parent adoption/pre-adoption.

liaison fostering officer	recruitment or licensing officer.
parental rights resolution	a legal provision, under review, in which the full parental rights of a child, originally admitted to care on a temporary voluntary basis, are transferred to the local authority.
residential care	group residential care.
residential key worker	group care worker who, in liaison with a child's caseworker, co-ordinates case management.
schedule	a research instrument for collecting data.
social worker/field social worker	caseworker.
social work team	group of caseworkers serving a locality (a 'team leader' is the senior member, or manager, of this group).
Social Services Department	a department of local government providing social work services for children, families, elderly, disabled, mentally ill, physically and mentally handicapped people.
vetting (as in 'foster home vetting')	assessing and approving.

It may also be helpful to explain that 'three-monthly', 'six-monthly', etc. refers to once in every three or six months, and not to three or six times *each* month.

Index